WHITE LIES

MAURICE BERGER

WHITE LIES

RACE AND THE MYTHS OF WHITENESS

FARRAR ■ STRAUS ■ GIROUX

NEW YORK

Farrar, Straus and Giroux
19 Union Square West, New York 10003

For Marvin Heiferman

The white man is sealed in his whiteness. The black man in his blackness.

—Frantz Fanon, *Black Skin, White Masks* (1952)

WHITE LIES

P R O L O G U E
(April 4, 1968)

Moments after a television news bulletin announced that Martin Luther King, Jr., was dead, my mother said he deserved to die. She rose up from the green sofa in the living room of our low-income apartment in the Lower East Side projects and began venting her grievances about the civil rights leader: He was a troublemaker. He was selfish and self-serving. He was poisoning the country. He was ungrateful to those brave and foolish white people who stood by his side in the civil rights movement. He was giving all the bigots in the South a reason to hate the good *schwartzes,* and the Jews, and anyone else who was not like them.

The things my mother said about Dr. King were not inconsistent with some of the other things she tried to teach my sister and me: that only light-skinned blacks were worthy of our attention and respect; that black people "smell like baked beans"; that black people were generally not as smart as white people; and that we should refer to black people as *schwartzes,* the Yiddish equivalent of "niggers." (Sometimes she would out-smart unsuspecting *schwartzes* by reverting to a secret code, known only to her and her children: she would instruct us to use the word *weisse,* or "whitey," whenever a black person was around, so that he would not know that we were talking about him.)

Confused and frightened by her tirade that night, I excused myself. As I walked down the hall to the bedroom I shared with my sister, I heard my father sobbing. He never watched TV with us; he would usually retreat to his bedroom after dinner, read the newspaper—*The New York Times* for the hard news, the *Post* for its liberal commentary—and listen to the radio. The door to his room was open; I walked in without knocking. He was crying so hard he was unable to speak. His behavior frightened me even more than my mother's. I was nearly twelve years old, and I had never seen my father cry. Tears rolled down his face as his finger pointed to the radio, which blared updates on the assassination. "What a nightmare," he finally muttered. I lay down next to him, put my head on his chest, and remained there for the rest of the evening.

M O T H E R

More than anything, my mother's life was shaped by her otherness: the darkness of her skin, eyes, and hair; her Sephardic heritage; her Hispanic-sounding maiden name. More than once she had been called a spic. More than once she had been called a kike, a hebe, a Jew bastard. More than once she had lost a job because a producer or casting director thought she was "too dark" or "too Jewish." My mother was the embodiment of the mutability of race, the evidence that terms like "black" and "white" are imprecise at best, living proof that miscegenation has blurred the racial boundaries of almost every one of us, confirmation that race itself is socially and culturally constructed.

In nineteenth-century America the law in many states would have qualified people lighter-skinned than my mother as black because of the traces of African blood that coursed through their veins. But by the 1920s my dark, small grandfather could slip past rigid quotas and through U. S. immigration as white on the basis of his word and the implied promise that he would strive to meet the immigrant ideal of an all-American whiteness.

My mother's earliest memories were shaped in an environment of prejudice and fear. She was born in Germany in 1920. Her father, Norbert Secunda, a research assistant in the mathematics department of the University of Hamburg, had confronted the usual bigotry known to Jews in Germany in the years before the rise of National Socialism. His projects at the university were often ignored or stripped of funding. The ranking members of his department, who, in polite conversation, would frequently refer to the fact that he was Jewish, encouraged him to find work elsewhere. Fearing that he would not survive this situation, he immigrated with his family to the United States in 1927, leaving behind a steady income and most of his worldly possessions. His fears were prescient. By the end of World War II, nearly every member of both his and his wife's families—scores of men, women, and children—had been killed by the Nazis.

Living in New York with her mother (her parents divorced soon after they immigrated), my mother decided to pursue a career as a singer. The prejudice she encountered played a significant role in undermining her professional life and destroying her morale. While she gave recitals at the Metropolitan Opera House, the old Brooklyn Paramount, and other venues in the late 1930s and early 1940s, her revered voice teacher, a retired soprano assigned through one of the programs of the Works

Progress Administration, was a destructive bigot and Jew hater. She continually warned my mother that if she did not convert to Roman Catholicism and capitalize on the "Spanish good looks" that would easily allow her to pass for Gentile, she would never make it in the professional opera world. My mother, an Orthodox Jew, would not even consider the idea. The teacher, initially one of my mother's greatest supporters, retaliated by relentlessly assigning Christian hymns (which my mother refused to sing), cutting back on her participation in student recitals, and refusing to write letters of reference or recommend her to agents and producers.

My mother's dark, ethnic looks frequently prevented her from getting roles, even bit parts, in the small theater companies she turned to after her opera career stalled in the 1940s. She changed her name to the all-American, professional-sounding Karen Grant after a number of agents and producers warned her that her given name, Ruth Secunda, sounded too exotic, too Spanish, too Jewish. (The name Secunda had achieved national prominence in the late 1930s after the Yiddish song "Bei Mir Bist du Schön," written by a relative of my mother, Sholom Secunda, became a hit for the Andrews Sisters.) After a brief stint in Miami in the late 1940s—where daily trips to the beach rendered her an even deeper shade of brown, leading producers to typecast her for roles in Latin nightclub revues—she returned to New York and took up work as a lingerie salesgirl. The only parts she could get were in the small Yiddish theater companies that still dotted Manhattan's Lower East Side.

My mother's career ended when she met and married my father in 1954. Broke and living on the Lower East Side with her obsessive, overbearing stage mother, she saw my father as a way out of her failed life. Listening to her scratchy old 78 rpm demonstration records years later, I realized that her voice—an amalgam of coloratura grace, overwrought emotion, and quivery vibrato—probably would not have made her a star. But I have never doubted that racism and anti-Semitism helped to undermine her self-image and her will. She would never forgive the bigots who she believed thwarted her professional life and forced her to trade a future on the stage for a life of poverty and hardship. Even on her deathbed, she found a way of blaming her terminal illness on prejudice. Medical researchers had long suspected that cancer was caused by repressed rage, she told me, and an early death was the price she was paying for years of buried anger against the Jew haters who had destroyed her life.

W H I T E

In May 1996, *Nightline* aired a weeklong series, "America in Black and White," on racial division in the United States. The first two episodes dealt with an incident that had occurred months earlier in the Bridesburg section of Philadelphia. Eight hours after an African American woman, Bridget Ward, moved into the white, working-class neighborhood with her two daughters, her home was vandalized. Racial epithets, including "Die Nigger Die" and "Leave Nigger Now," were scrawled on her front steps and ketchup was splattered to simulate blood. Although some white neighbors went to Ward's house to apologize and welcome her to the community, others were featured on local and national TV news programs spewing racist venom: "It's against the law, but if they get them out, that's fine" . . . "Bluebirds don't mix with robins" . . . "She should have expected trouble. Nobody wants mixed people in their neighborhood." Ward was given twenty-four-hour police protection and a police escort for her children. Two weeks later, she received an anonymous letter threatening violent damage to her house. Disgusted and fearing for her family's safety, she decided to move out of Bridesburg. "I don't need all these hateful people around me," she concluded.

Nightline followed up its report on this incident with a mini town meeting in which a small group of the neighborhood's white residents answered questions posed by the show's host, Ted Koppel. Respondents, at times, seemed tentative and unsure of their feelings. One woman felt at once ashamed and afraid of her racist neighbors and apprehensive about the possibility that black people might bring crime to the neighborhood. The group, however, could not agree on how much racism there was in Bridesburg. One man, responding to another's claim that Bridesburg was home to "many people of color," reminded his neighbors that the community of six thousand had only a handful of black residents. When another man declared that the "thing we want in this neighborhood is good people" without regard to their race, one woman snickered in disbelief. One man snapped back that race *was* the issue for most residents. "Why lie about it?" he asked.

The anxiety that many in the group appeared to share was that integration might endanger the integrity and future of Bridesburg. As Ted Koppel summed it up: "I've heard fears expressed . . . that what you are concerned about is . . . that the community you've established, the safety you've established, the property values you've established could in some way be damaged if African American families were to start moving in . . .

You've cited other communities in the Philadelphia area where you say that has happened and it has caused the whole community to go downhill."

On the second night's broadcast, Koppel ventured deeper into the race question. If blackness could depreciate the value of their community, he asked, was their own whiteness, conversely, in some way valuable? Starting from the premise that skin color is not something white people dwell on in the United States, Koppel wondered if whites just don't understand the difference between living one's life free of racial prejudice and constantly dodging the bullets, both large and small, of racism. A *Nightline* poll confirmed this suspicion: while 75 percent of black respondents agreed with the statement that "blacks and other minorities [were] discriminated against in housing," only 44 percent of whites held this view.

To shift the attention of the group toward a more self-conscious assessment of their own racial attitudes, Koppel asked a question that was a variation on a classroom exercise designed by Queens College professor Andrew Hacker more than twenty years earlier. Hacker proposed a hypothetical situation to his white students: It is now the future, and you find out that a government agency and not genetics determined your race and the race of every baby born in the United States over the past number of years. One morning, a representative of this government agency responsible for determining race comes to your house to inform you that you were born the wrong color and within hours would be involuntarily returned to your proper race. The government has set aside some money, he tells you, that it offers as grants to help people in your situation adjust to your new racial status. How much economic compensation, Hacker asked, would you seek if you were changed from white to black? "How much do you want?" Koppel asked his group of white respondents. "How much would it take?"

With this provocative question, the group's understanding of the power relationships of race seemed to shift. People who moments earlier had denied that racism was a problem in Bridesburg now were willing to concede that being black in America might be more difficult than being white. "I would take $50 million, then I could live anywhere. I wouldn't have to deal with any racism," remarked one man. "I'd rather be white," interjected another. "It's easier. I admit that it's easier to be white. I admit that blacks got a bad hand dealt to them." In this role-playing exercise, while most respondents insisted that it was not being black, per se, but the government's mistake and the problems associated with adjusting to a new race that merited them lavish compensation, each clearly saw his or her whiteness as an advantage.

P O W D E R

From the time I was a little boy, I kept Mother company as she made herself up in the morning. She felt comfortable letting me in on this feminine ritual. Her half-hour-long "beauty regimen," as she called it, was fascinating and, as she whipped out an assortment of vials and brushes, theatrical. She fixed herself rigidly before the mirror and began. First, she would brush her jet-black hair, applying gobs of foul-smelling, viscous pomades in an effort to relax her tight, kinky curls into gentle waves. She would apply Lancôme or Shiseido moisturizer to her skin, followed by concealer under her eyes and on freckles and moles, liquid foundation many shades lighter than her olive complexion, and a dusting of chalky face powder. She would draw on her lips with pencil and fill in the outline with bright-red lipstick. Finally, she would spray her neck and hair liberally with perfume, favoring heavy, intoxicating fragrances like Tabu and

Fiji. She would turn away from the mirror and face me only after her makeup was in place and her hair was properly coiffed. I would tell her how beautiful she looked. Then, and only then, was she able to show herself to the rest of the world.

P O W E R

Kerry Michaels, a writer and television producer tells, this story:

It was 1985, and I was going to travel around Kenya by myself before visiting my brother, who was working for the U.S. Centers for Disease Control in Malawi. I had only a vague idea of what I was going to do in Kenya. Having traveled all night, I arrived, exhausted and a little nervous, at the Nairobi airport at about five in the morning.

The terminal was a big, square hall—very austere, very official-looking. I glanced up. There was a balcony that ran all around the room. Standing on this balcony at perfect intervals were the blackest men I had ever seen in my life. They wore olive-drab uniforms and crimson berets. They all held rifles across their chests. They made an incredibly powerful, aesthetically stunning image: regal posture, beautiful, chiseled black faces, caps all cocked at the same angle.

I know this might sound stupid, but as I, a white American woman in my late twenties, looked around the airport, I realized that the power structure was black. The customs officials were black. The security officials examining my passport were black. Everyone who controlled my fate was black. It occurred to me what it was truly like to be a minority (albeit, when you are white in Africa, an empowered minority). In New York, if you're the only white person on the subway, you're still not a minority, because the power structure around you is white. In the Nairobi airport, I realized how different it was to have the power reside in a different race. It was the black men who were holding the guns. The government they served was black. The idea that the whole country was being run by black people was absolutely alien to me. To be white and find myself situated at the bottom of this massive hall, with these black men standing with guns over my head, really gave me a sense of what this inversion of power feels like. Why had I never realized this before? You think that as a white liberal you get it. But you don't.

S M I L E

As a child, I wasn't sure what to make of my mother's view of black people. I tended to excuse her ideas as embarrassing quirks, as odd miscalculations of a world I experienced differently and daily, a world of black neighbors, black classmates, black teachers. It was precisely this world that my mother struggled to transcend. She found remarkable ways to keep clear of black people. She would avoid looking at the people she did not want to see. She would make small talk with people she did not want to hear. She would change the subject from the things she did not want to think about. (Her two "friends" in the projects both lived on our floor: an elderly Jewish widow, Mrs. Schwartz, and a light-skinned Puerto Rican woman, Mrs. Salgada—the kind of Hispanic person my mother would refer to as "white Spanish." Neither woman was ever invited into our apartment.) My mother was the strange lady with the brightly colored dresses who politely nodded hello, averted her eyes, and kept walking. Her lips would curl up into a false, inscrutable smile. No one would ever know the contempt she felt for them. Or so she believed.

PROBLEM

They approach me in a half-hesitant sort of way, eye me curiously or compassionately, and then instead of saying directly, How does it feel to be a problem? they say, I know an excellent colored man in my town . . . Do not these Southern outrages make your blood boil? At these, I smile, or am interested, or reduce the boiling to a simmer, as the occasion may require. To the real question, How does it feel to be a problem? I answer seldom a word. *

■

[Liberals] relieve their guilty consciences by supporting public funds directed at "the problems" [of black people]; but at the same time, reluctant to exercise principled criticism of black people, liberals deny them the

* W.E.B. Du Bois, *The Souls of Black Folk* (1903).

1 9

freedom to err. Similarly, conservatives blame the "problems" on black people themselves—and thereby render black social misery invisible or unworthy of public attention . . . [F]or liberals, black people are to be "included" and "integrated" in "our" society and culture, while for conservatives they are to be "well-behaved" and "worthy of acceptance" by "our" way of life. Both fail to see that the presence and predicaments of black people are neither additions to nor defections from American life, but rather constitute elements of that life.*

It's being constantly reminded that you're different, that you're not good enough, that you have to prove yourself, that you have to be better than average, just to be considered normal . . . I am to the point now where when someone has a problem with my race, or my color, or my ability to be a human, and they only see me as an object, a black guy, a "blackie," I deal with it. When they have a problem, I leave it as their problem. I make sure that they understand that this problem that they're having is only theirs. If they have a problem with how I look, who I am, then maybe they should stop looking at me, stop associating with me.†

---

* Cornel West, *Race Matters* (1993).

† Anonymous young black man, a recent college graduate, in a Western city, as quoted by Joe R. Feagin and Melvin P. Sikes, in *Living with Racism: The Black Middle-Class Experience* (1994).

NEGRO LOVER

I was six years old and walking with my mother through the main square of the Baruch Houses—walkways, benches, lawns, all arranged around a central flagpole. The small park was relatively clean and neatly manicured. I ran over to one of the low fences and threw a pebble onto the lawn behind it. A housing-authority employee—a bearded white man—came running over to my mother. He warned her about keeping an eye on me. It was against the law, he reminded her, for anyone to throw anything onto the grass. He pointed to the KEEP OFF THE GRASS sign. My mother reminded him that I wasn't on the grass when I threw the stone. He told me he would call the police if he ever again caught me "defacing" the lawn. "The grass belongs to *everyone* who lives in the project, not just you," he said. My mother, enraged, now asked the man if he would have said anything had her child been black. She accused him of being an "ass kisser," a "Negro lover" who coddled Negroes because he was secretly afraid of them. "If my son was colored," she growled at him, "you would have turned the other cheek."

B E A U T Y

1

His tall, well-proportioned body is graceful and athletic. His face, with its square jaw and high cheekbones, is perfectly symmetrical. He is at once typical and perfect. Modeled from an averaging of the measurements of thousands of "native white" men gathered from many parts of the United States, he is a life-size composite of ideal data translated into three dimensions. A model of "normal" perfection—Dr. Robert Latou Dickinson calculated his proportions and posture, and the artist Abram Belskie sculpted his perfect form—he has been named Norman. And along with his perfect sister, Norma, he stands as a testament to the character and attractiveness of the American nationality. Norma and Norman evoke the psychotic enterprise of the Nazi geneticists who searched for statistics to prove their claims of Aryan superiority and beauty. But back in 1945, when the results of Dickinson and Belskie's work were published and illustrated in *Natural History* magazine, most readers accepted their conclusions without questioning them. Norma and Norman exemplified the ability of the cold, hard, irrefutable "objectivity" of science to arrive at a truth that could help make the United States a better place.

2

Everything, everywhere I look, everywhere I turn, right, left, is white. It's lily white, it's painted with white. And it's funny, because I was reading this article about how America is synonymous with white people. I mean, I'm sure when Europeans, or Asians, or Africans for that matter, think of America, they think of white people, because white people are mainstream, white people are general. "White is right," as my daddy tells me. White is right, at least they think it is . . . Everything this country stands for is what is white.*

3

"The beauty of the female face," *The New York Times* told us in an article on the front page of the August 5, 1986, science section, " . . . is mathematically quantifiable." Researcher Michael Cunningham, a psychologist at the University of Louisville in

---

* Unnamed black student at a historically white university, as quoted in *Living with Racism.*

Kentucky, mapped the female face in order to measure what men saw as most attractive. The *Times* described his method as follows: "150 white, male American college students [were asked] to rate the attractiveness and social attributes of 50 women from pictures of their faces. Twenty-seven of the women were finalists in the Miss Universe contest . . . [M]ost of the women were white." According to the *Times*, specific features, "some determined within millimeters," became important markers of female beauty. Dimensions and proportions of what was regarded as attractive, the scientist maintained, emerged with "remarkable consistency." (The most attractive distance from the center of the eye to the bottom of the face, for example, was one-tenth the height of the body.) Rather than positing an ideal face or absolute beauty, Dr. Cunningham's data resulted in a "developed standard"—a way to "describe the images that a culture, in this case the American culture, defines as attractive." This "blueprint for beauty," according to the schematic rendering of the perfect female face that accompanied the article, had straight hair, light skin, almond-shaped eyes, thin, arched eyebrows, a long, narrow nose, closely set and tiny nostrils, a large mouth, and thin lips.

4

I am having dinner with a colleague and his new girlfriend. She is a white woman in her mid-fifties, who teaches in a racially mixed elementary school in Boston. She tells me that she grew up in a racist neighborhood and has fought all her life not to be racist. She tells me that she "loves" President Clinton's idea of a "national conversation on race," because she believes that it is only through getting to know each other that we can fight our racist tendencies. I ask her if the faculty of her school is racially mixed. She tells me that it is and that she is learning a great deal about black people from her African American colleagues. She tells me about a black teacher she has befriended and mentored, a much younger woman who teaches art. She tells me almost nothing about her colleague except that she is physically attractive. "You know black women *can* be very beautiful sometimes," she says proudly.

5

Superstar author-model-actress Naomi Campbell is crying foul over her positioning in the latest issue of Vogue, *which consigns the black beauty to the magazine's gatefold while fresh-faced Florida blonde Niki Taylor graces the cover. Naomi, it seems, was under the impression that she was to be May's cover girl, and considers her abrupt relocation to the magazine's inner cover a suspicious dis . . . Other models of color have long complained about the scarcity of their kind at* Vogue, *which hasn't put a black model on its cover in more than two years. "I'm conditioned to this," says Bethann Hardison, a modeling agent and founder of the Black Girls Coalition. "They're not going to put the black girl on the front and the blonde girl inside . . ."* *

* Beth Landman and Deborah Mitchell, "Naomi Goes Under Cover at *Vogue*" (*New York,* May 6, 1996).

In the spring of 1998, Timothy Egan of *The New York Times* reported that one of the oldest archaeological finds of human remains in North America had been given a face. As reconstructed by anthropologist James Chatters, the clay bust of the ninety-three-hundred-year-old face of the "Kennewick Man" closely resembled the actor Patrick Stewart, who appeared in *Star Trek: The Next Generation* at the time. The anthropological casting provoked a bitter debate around the issue of race and the question of the racial origins of America's earliest peoples.

A number of anthropologists charged that in giving a late-Pleistocene-era skull the face of a contemporary British actor Dr. Chatters assigned a racial identification to a creature that may be impossible to categorize racially. Dr. Chatters initially theorized that the skull belong to an early white settler. But through radiocarbon dating scientists concluded that the bones long predated the arrival of white people in America. Dr. Chatters and two associates ultimately characterized the skull as "Caucasoid" because in their view it did not have any Indian features. "Nobody is talking white here," Chatters said in an address to the Sixty-third Annual Meeting of the American Society of Archaeology. "We're just talking about physical characteristics." When later asked why he made the skull look like a white man, and in particular like Patrick Stewart, Dr. Chatters said that as he tried to visualize the skull the *Star Trek* actor most strongly came to mind.

*Adults, older girls, shops, magazines, newspapers, window signs—all the world had agreed that a blue-eyed, yellow-haired, pink-skinned doll was what every girl child treasured. "Here," they said, "this is beautiful, and if you are on this day 'worthy' you may have it." I fingered the face, wondering at the single-stroke eyebrows; picked at the pearly teeth stuck like two piano keys between red bowline lips. Traced the turned-up nose, poked the glassy blue eyeballs, twisted the yellow hair. I could not love it. But I could examine it to see what it was that all the world said was lovable. Break off the tiny fingers, bend the flat feet, loosen the hair, twist the head around, and the thing made one sound—a sound they said was the sweet and plaintive cry "Mama," but which sounded to me like the bleat of a dying lamb, or, more precisely, our icebox door opening on rusty hinges in July. Remove the cold and stupid eyeball, it would bleat still, "Ahhhhhh," take off the head, shake out the sawdust, crack the back against the brass bed rail, it would bleat still. The gauze back would split, and I could see the disk with six holes, the secret of the sound. A mere metal roundness.**

* Toni Morrison, *The Bluest Eye* (1970).

SILENCE

Antonia Gardner, a writer and editor, tells this story:

Because of my father's job, we moved often throughout Alabama and Florida when I was a kid. For the fourth grade, in 1962, I lived in Tuscaloosa, Alabama. There was one child in my all-white class whom we all were wary of; I had immediately noticed that he was different. In those days, boys wore button-down shirts and trousers. Bobby Shelton wore dungarees—clean and stiff, with thick, neat, rolled-up cuffs—and a clean white T-shirt, which to me was purely underwear. Blue jeans were work clothes then, not something to wear to school, not standard clothing for middle- and upper-middle-class children. He was the smallest boy in class, wiry, with pale skin, milky-blue eyes, and a tight, blond crew cut. His fists were perpetually clenched; he was always picking fights with everyone.

Years later I came across a short article on Robert Shelton, my classmate's father. Shelton was stepping down as the Grand

Imperial Dragon or Wizard or whatever it was called. It was really amazing: here was the son of the Imperial Wizard—the top Klansman in America—and with the exception of my best friend, who had whispered a rumor in my ear about Mr. Shelton, nobody back in Tuscaloosa ever talked about who Bobby's father was. The Klan was a frightening presence in our lives but wasn't discussed openly. Educated, tolerant white people who were contemptuous of the Klan were also afraid of it; they knew that its members were just as likely to go after white civil rights sympathizers. There was the sneaky, furtive, ominous silence of the Klan, and there was the polite and frightened silence of everyone else.

But whites were afraid of more than just the Klan; their silence extended to all questions of race and racism. I can't recall hearing negative remarks about black people, only oblique references to "troubles." Some were annoying. We couldn't go downtown sometimes, for example, because of demonstrations. Other events were more sinister. An acquaintance of my parents in Anniston, who owned the local newspaper, had his kids' lives threatened and a cross burned on his lawn for publishing pro–civil rights articles. But these things were not spoken of openly; you picked up information in bits. The day Autherine Lucy entered the University of Alabama as its first black student, for example, my mother thought the traffic jam was for a football game, there had been so little local conversation or press.

Race was part of everyday life, yet, at least among the children, it was never discussed. We didn't talk about black people in general terms or civil rights or the local race problems. Our lives were mostly separate from those issues. At home, my parents would tell me a bit of it—literacy tests, for example, which they saw as bizarre. But no one thought of fighting these wrongs. They were simply described as part of the unjust ways things were, the ironies of life.

In town, I would approach water fountains and find WHITES ONLY signs, with smaller fountains and smaller COLORED signs nearby; I would back off from them with a queasy feeling but never say anything about it. Even a child could feel that this was weird and wrong, but it seemed to be the odd order of the grownup world. I also knew I was lucky. I would smell the paper mill's putrid fumes in the morning and know that by noon the stench would be gone from my neighborhood. I also knew it would settle in the poorer white and colored neighborhoods, poisoning the air with its sulfur, and I'd heave a secret sigh of relief, knowing that I didn't have to live there.

DELUSION

One must be careful not to take refuge in any delusion—and the value placed on the color of the skin is always and everywhere and forever a delusion.

—James Baldwin, *The Fire Next Time*

In *The End of Racism,* the neoconservative social critic Dinesh D'Souza argues that liberals have exaggerated both the history and persistence of racism in America. In his view, many race activists—the politicians, academics, and bureaucrats he refers to as "race merchants"—are poisoning the minds of a younger generation that is less bigoted and race conscious than any other in American history. Racism, D'Souza claims, is no longer the main problem confronting blacks. To demonstrate how far America has come in this regard, he cites for the purpose of comparison a list of popular stereotypes and prejudices about blacks published in George Jean Nathan and H. L. Mencken's *The American Credo* (1920):

- Negroes who are intelligent are always part white
- Negro parties always end up in bloody brawls

- Negroes who have money head straight for the dentist to have their front teeth filled with gold
- Illiterate Negroes labor hard but educated Negroes lose all interest in work
- Negro prize fighters marry white women and then beat them
- Negroes will sell their votes for a dollar

The list is typical of early-twentieth-century racial prejudices. What is extraordinary, however, is D'Souza's accompanying claim: "As the widespread popularity of African Americans such as Colin Powell, Bill Cosby, and Michael Jordan illustrates, none of these beliefs seems to be held today by any measurable degree of the population." Although D'Souza's reasoning is specious—one cannot necessarily conclude that the popularity of a few black people bespeaks a nation that is free of racist taint—it is driven by a durable myth: that the worst of American racism lies comfortably in the past. The author, an American of East Indian descent, is essentially telling his white readers that there is nothing of themselves to be seen in Nathan and Mencken's diatribe.

Quite to the contrary, however, most of these earlier stereotypes have counterparts in contemporary culture:

- *Negroes who are intelligent are always part white:* Richard Herrnstein and Charles Murray's controversial and widely debated book, *The Bell Curve,* brought out by D'Souza's own publisher in 1994, argues that blacks are *genetically* predisposed to do less well on IQ tests than whites.

• *Negro parties always end up in bloody brawls:* The most violent, dangerous, or criminal aspects of black ghetto life often are employed manipulatively by Republican and Democratic strategists alike to play on the race-related fears of white voters—from congressional attacks on lurid rap-music lyrics to the highly effective use in a 1988 Republican Presidential campaign commercial of the menacing mug shot of a black criminal who raped and murdered white people while out on a weekend furlough.

• *Negroes who have money head straight for the dentist to have their front teeth filled with gold:* Rather than offering thoughtful analyses of the problems and triumphs of the black "underclass," the media often portray poorer African Americans as wasting their precious dollars on such status symbols as gold jewelry and expensive sneakers.

• *Negro prize fighters marry white women and then beat them:* It is doubtful that the O. J. Simpson trial would have been the "trial of the century" had the murder victim been Simpson's first wife, who was black.

• *Negroes will sell their votes for a dollar:* In 1993, New Jersey Republican Governor-elect Christine Todd Whitman's campaign manager boasted to the press that the campaign had paid black ministers cash to encourage their parishioners, most of them Democrats, to stay home on election day—a claim later retracted by him and debunked by a federal investigation.

D'Souza charts the underlying reasons for racist thinking in the 1920s—that white myths about black intelligence, for example, were "strengthened by the observed preponderance of light-skinned mulattos in the black middle class" or that the wild reputation of black boxers was kindled by "the flamboyant experience of Jack Johnson, who raised controversy . . . when he married a white woman"—but disavows their legacy in the 1990s. He bases his evaluations on a literal-minded, black-and-white comparison between the brutal, unreconstructed racism of the past and the undeniable civil rights advances of recent years. But although Jim Crow segregation does not exist anymore, its underlying belief systems have not disappeared. What is missing from D'Souza's reasoning is the idea that earlier forms of overt racism have mutated into less strident, less obvious forms in response to decades of antidiscrimination laws and changing sensitivities.

What is most dangerous about the myth of racism's impending end is that it fosters a false sense of complacency and assurance. At a time when the problems of racism are clearly not about to disappear, falling back on the myth that things are so much better than they used to be seems ill-advised. Yet D'Souza's travels through the American racial landscape suggest to him that white Americans can relax and stop obsessing over sins long since atoned for. In the end, the things he has elected to see, living in an "integrated" society, lead him to think that white people's negative generalizations about black people may not be so wrong after all. Liberal ideologues, he argues, have either ignored or excused the cultural pathologies and "civilizational" inferiorities of black Americans. D'Souza concludes, two paragraphs down from Nathan and Mencken's litany of Negro traits and weaknesses, that there is a fundamental problem with the liberal antiracist paradigm:

> its premise that all group perceptions are misperceptions: that every negative generalization about blacks is automatically false and the product of distorted projections. Paradoxically, it is desegregation and integration which have now called the liberal paradigm into question. One of the risks of increased exposure to blacks is that it has placed whites in a position to discover which of their preconceived views about blacks are true. Education and integration can help to dispel erroneous judgments about groups but they are only likely to reinforce accurate ones.

TRASH

Jew bastard. Lousy Christ killer," screamed Anthony, my second-grade classmate, as he split open the skin on the top of my head with a wooden broom handle. Anthony was the class troublemaker, a wiry Italian American kid given to using racial and ethnic slurs instead of proper names. (Until the white flight of the mid-1960s, a small number of white students attended the public school adjacent to the Lower East Side project where I lived.) A scrawny and nerdy yeshiva boy, I was Anthony's perfect prey. He was always saying he was going to beat me up and now he had finally made good on his threats. As I sat on the classroom floor dazed and crying, my hands bloodied from touching my wounded scalp, the teacher sent Anthony to the principal's office.

The next few weeks were harrowing: my mother demanding that we sue; my father warning that trials were usually ugly and futile; visits to the attorney's and doctor's offices; guilty entreaties from the teacher who had ignored my fears that Anthony was going to hurt me and who left her class unattended while he did; a long sermon-like apology delivered by an obsequious school principal fearful of a lawsuit. In the end, my father prevailed and my parents, convinced that anti-Semitism was involved, decided to appeal to local Hebrew schools. The head rabbi of the East Side Hebrew Institute took pity on my sister and me and accepted us as students, mid-semester, with full scholarships.

It was at this day school where I learned most dramatically what it felt like to be an outsider, because most of its students came from the neatly manicured, middle-class cooperative developments that dotted the Lower East Side. The projects were these kids' worst nightmare, pits of darkness and poverty out of which their parents had climbed just a few years earlier. From the start, teachers assumed my sister and I were dull-witted or impaired; classmates whispered rumors that we were "dirty," "smelly," "weird," "stupid," and "strange." In our three years at the school, we were never invited to a classmate's birthday party. My only friend for the first year was the fattest boy in school; my sister's was the fattest girl. We formed a kind of losers' club, sharing in an unbalanced diet of meanness and ostracism.

We were ultimately forced out of the East Side Hebrew Institute. The head rabbi informed my mother that I had a "serious reading problem." His evaluation struck her as particularly odd. She had taught me to read before I was in kindergarten; by the third grade I was reading the newspaper every evening. My teacher had observed that while other kids were reading the assignment I would look up from my book after a few minutes and "daydream." My mother suggested that I be tested; the rabbi refused.

A year later the institute administered a standardized school-wide reading exam. I scored the highest in my class. Boredom rather than a learning disorder was the reason for my "problem." The rabbi's response was swift and decisive: he rescinded our scholarships, claiming that my sister's relatively low reading scores no longer qualified us for financial support. (I, on the other hand, had scored four years beyond my grade level.) My unemployed father was faced with the impossible task of coming up with next year's tuition by the end of the summer. He couldn't, and my sister and I returned to public school that fall, surprised, and strangely relieved, to find that nearly all the white kids had moved away.

W H I T E [2]

Once I asked my part Irish–part Native American mother, who had grown up orphaned and homeless in foster homes as a servant and in a reformatory, why my father's family name, Dunbar, was shared by a black person. In my high school English class we had just read some poems by the African American poet Paul Laurence Dunbar. I hoped my mother would say he was a relative of ours. But she said that my Dunbar ancestors were "Scotch Irish" and had once owned huge plantations and many slaves and that the slaves took the names of the masters.

"How do we know we are related to the masters and not the slaves?" I asked.

"Because you are white," she answered, closing the discussion forever.*

---

* Roxanne A. Dunbar, "Bloody Footprints: Reflections on Growing Up Poor White," in *White Trash: Race and Class in America* (1997).

■

In the 1970s, Doug Daniels, a sociology professor at the University of Regina in Canada, devised an informal questionnaire in order to test his students' perceptions of which national groups were white and which were not. Almost all his students were Caucasian. "I'm going to read you a list of names of different nationalities. I want you to tell me whether you think they are 'white' people or not. Don't stop and think about it—I don't want your scientific opinion but just what we absorb from our popular culture. Just pretend you're on a psychologist's couch doing word associations and answer as quickly as possible."

Daniels tabulated the results of the questionnaire over an eight-year period, and they remained startlingly consistent. Here is his list:

Who is white?
List of nationalities

Swedes   Yes
Congolese   No
Canadians   Yes
Icelanders   Yes
Spaniards   Slow yes, or some nos
Belgians   Yes
Dutch   Yes
Turks   No (very rare yes)
Germans   Yes
Algerians   No
English   Yes

Welsh   Yes
Cubans   No
Danes   Yes
Israelis   Yes (an occasional no)
Chileans   No (very few "yes" replies)
Ugandans   No
Scots   Yes
Americans   Yes
Japanese   No (a very occasional yes)
Swiss   Yes
Portuguese   hesitation, half of class unsure, most of
   remainder say "no"
Poles   Yes
Russians   Yes
Mexicans   90% no, 10% yes
Arabs   No
Argentineans   80% no, 20% yes
Finns   Yes
Bulgarians   30% yes, 70% don't know
Norwegians   Yes
Italians   hesitation, 50% yes, 50% no
Chinese   No
Moroccans   80% no, 20% yes
Egyptians   60% no, 20% yes, rest undecided
Iranians   No (100%)
Greeks   Yes (after some hesitation)
Vietnamese   No
Quebecois   Laughter
Ukrainians   (Laughter) Yes

■

If we may safely judge by the army measurements of intelligence, races are quite significantly different as individuals . . . [and] almost as great as the intellectual differences between Negro and white in the army are the differences between white racial groups . . .

For the past ten years or so the intellectual status of immigrants has been disquietingly low. Perhaps this is because of the dominance of the Mediterranean races, as contrasted with the Nordic and Alpine.*

■

The racialization of Eastern Europeans was likewise striking. White racist jokes mocked the black servant who thought her child, fathered by a Chinese man, would be a Jew, racist folklore held that Jews, inside-out, were "niggers." In 1926, Serbo-Croatians ranked near the bottom of a list of forty "ethnic" groups whom "white American" respondents were asked to order according to the respondents' willingness to associate with members of each group. They placed just above Negroes, Filipinos, and Japanese. Just above them were Poles, who were near the middle of the list. One sociologist has recently written that "a good many groups on this color continuum [were] not considered white by a large number of Americans."†

---

* Psychologist Robert Yerkes, a proponent of eugenics, writing in *The Atlantic Monthly* in 1923; as quoted by Lewis H. Carlson and George A. Colburn, in *In Their Place: White America Defines Her Minorities, 1850–1950* (1972).
† James R. Barrett and David Roediger, "How White People Became White," in *Critical White Studies: Looking Behind the Mirror* (1997).

There is Italian culture, and Polish, Irish, Yiddish, German, and Appalachian culture: There is youth culture and drug culture and queer culture; but there is no "white" culture—unless you mean Wonder Bread and television game shows. Whiteness is nothing but an expression of race privilege. It has been said that the typical "white" American male spends his childhood as an Indian, his adolescence as an Afro-American, and only becomes white when he reaches the age of legal responsibility.*

* Noel Ignatiev, "Treason to Whiteness Is Loyalty to Humanity" (*The Blast!*, June/July 1994).

R A G E

Shirley Verrett, a soprano, tells this story:

It was 1970. I was at a rehearsal in a major European city for a concert version of an opera. I was the only American singer in the production, and Americans, supposedly the best-prepared singers, were very much sought after in Europe at that time. In the Baroque music we were singing, there is something called appoggiatura—grace notes that are used to create a more elegant finish to musical phrases or the ends of musical sentences. All of the composers of opera, up until the Romantic period, favored these grace notes. In my studies, I was trained to use them. At the rehearsal, I was the only singer employing them and respecting the musical practice of the time.

The conductor had clearly noticed what I was doing. He announced, "Madame Verrett's singing the score differently." He did not know the correct form and consequently did not follow my lead. He didn't ask me why I was singing the way I was. Instead, he asked the European singers, but not me, to explain to him the "right way" to sing these passages. I held my ground. Even though he didn't ask me, I immediately told him where my authority to interpret the music this way came from.

Clearly, the conductor was assuming that I, a black American woman, could not be correct. After all, how would a black woman know? Had I been a white American, he would have handled the problem more respectfully. He might have said: "I noticed you are using grace notes here. Could we talk about that?" His actions made me very angry. I was later vindicated by the European press, when the reviews for the concert came out and I was the only performer credited with singing the music correctly.

Incidents like this take me back to my childhood. When I was a little girl, my father relocated the family from New Orleans to California, because he did not want us ever to feel that we were second-class citizens. While he wanted us to know what was happening—the lynchings and other unspeakable acts that haunted black life in the South—he did not want us to develop what he called a "chip on our shoulder." I vividly remember the bigotry of the South. Even after we moved to California, we sometimes returned to the South on trips, and everywhere we went, we felt like criminals.

As a child and adolescent, I was violently angry about this bigotry. I wished a bomb could have just blown all the benighted, cruel people away. I was angry each time we were treated as second-class citizens, as if we didn't belong anywhere. I was angry when we weren't allowed to go into certain stores or to try on clothes because the fitting room was for whites only. I was angry when we had to go around to back doors to buy food or had to eat in the car because we couldn't be served in a restaurant. I was angry when we had to drink from separate water fountains. But I kept the fury bottled up inside.

As I got older, I realized that many white people were involved in the struggle for civil rights and that a bomb was not the answer. But the conductor's behavior brought me right back to my childhood rage. I had studied for four years at the Juilliard School of Music. I studied with the best coaches in the world. From the beginning of my career, I have always been associated with the very best institutions. I had sung with the finest con-ductors. I was furious that I once again had to answer for my musicality because I was black. This has happened many times, of course, and every time it does, I feel, at least for a moment, like a second-class citizen.

MENTOR

I was fourteen years old when Mrs. Mosley was my ninth-grade social studies and homeroom teacher in 1970. My adolescent view of age gave me no clue to how old Miriam Mosley was at the time. She could have been forty or sixty. In hindsight I remember that she had traces of gray hair on her temples; the rest of her very short Afro was black. I knew only what she let me know: that she had two sons; that she lived in East Orange, New Jersey; that she commuted daily to school by train, subway, and bus. She was tall and slender, with a physical awkwardness that reminded me of Eleanor Roosevelt. Her speaking voice was deep and precise, as if every word, every idea, every emotion mattered.

In the classroom, Mrs. Mosley taught American, European, and African history. She was my favorite teacher and, with the exception of my father, the smartest person I had ever known.

After school, she would often talk with me, sometimes for hours, about myriad subjects and questions, from Saharan weather patterns to the war in Vietnam. Intellectually, she pushed me hard, insisting I follow her example and examine any issue from as many sides as possible. Even racism, she once told me, had many moral dimensions.

Mrs. Mosley was the first person to teach me about Africa and, besides my father, the only person to talk with me about African American life and culture and about racism. Once, when I was telling her how angry it made me that black people still faced prejudice every day, she suggested that I try to understand the motivations of the bigot and not just the suffering of the victim. There was only one subject that Mrs. Mosley would not discuss: her own experiences, as a black person, with prejudice. Although she said that she had encountered painful, even violent racism in her life, she offered no stories, no details.

H A I R

Throughout my childhood, my mother used to tell my sister and me a story (or joke, I was never really sure) which she felt proved that black people were jealous of white people's beauty. When my mother was in the sixth grade, she sat in front of a black girl named Ima Payne. Ima (pronounced *eye-mah*), my mother would remind us, was a *mieskeit* (Yiddish for an "ugliness"), with "big lips and hopelessly kinky hair." She coveted my mother's "fair skin" and "long, wavy auburn" tresses. So jealous was Ima that she developed the habit of pulling on my mother's hair during class. "Ima just couldn't deal with my beauty," my mother would tell me. "How unfortunate that her name matched her personality."

C L A S S

In her book *The Rooster's Egg,* legal scholar Patricia J. Williams offers several examples of the ways economic class matters when white people assess their black colleagues and acquaintances. More often than not, she observes, white people force black people into neatly compartmentalized categories of class. In one instance, a candidate for a high Massachusetts public office publicly asks why he should bother to go campaigning among the "welfare mothers and drug addicts" of Roxbury. Roxbury, however, is not the decrepit ghetto of his fantasy; it is, in fact, a fairly sedate, middle-class black community. In another story, Williams recalls that after listening to a presentation by Harvard Law School professor Charles Ogletree, who is black, a white colleague asked her whether the man could have known *anything* about poverty. "Let's be real," the colleague insisted, "he teaches at Harvard." Williams knew Professor Ogletree understood poverty all too well, having grown up in a family of migrant field workers.

White people are often invested in the myth that African Americans either are impoverished or belong to an elite of celebrities, politicians, and athletes. In this mythic, either-or view of black life, African Americans are rarely understood to share the middle- and working-class allegiances of most whites. Such myths about race and class selectively come into play to disguise or justify negative or ambivalent views of blackness. Williams writes:

> "Most" blacks are middle class when the analysis is convenient: the huge, teeming, overemployed, better-than-ever-off middle class, demanding, insistent, arrogant—dismissed in many of the terms abounding in the rhetoric of anti-Semitism. Then in a flick of the eye, "most" blacks are underclass: innumerably teeming, underemployed, better-off-than-the-poor-anywhere-on-earth, yet demanding, insistent, cheating and arrogant—dismissed in the same old rhetoric of racism.

African Americans rarely escape these stereotypes. Well-meaning white people, trying to fit their black acquaintances and colleagues into "some preconceived box of blackness," often search for the ghetto child behind the successful adult. The writer and editor Brent Staples, for example, suspected what he was really being asked about his past when he was interviewed for a job with *The Washington Post:* "[The interviewer] wanted to know if I was a faux, Chevy Chase, Maryland, Negro or an authentic Nigger who grew up in the ghetto besieged by crime and violence. White people preferred the latter, on the theory that blacks from the ghetto were the real thing." Williams herself remembers being asked about her background by one of her white students, culminating in the bizarre question of whether the house she had grown up in was freestanding.

The comforting idea of the black middle class—an amorphous designation into which other economic categories of black life in America, from working class to wealthy, are merged—allows white people to distance themselves from their own racist feelings. White people often think that middle-class blacks no longer suffer the indignities of prejudice. Unlike their less fortunate ghetto brothers and sisters, the reasoning goes, middle-class blacks have economic and social standing to insulate them from crude attacks, insults, and slights. As Williams suggests, white people point to the black middle class to comfort themselves with the notion that racism isn't so bad anymore, that "but for a few rabble-rousing rioters . . . the black middle class is so darn happy, so well-off, so privileged it positively *whines.*"

Extending this idea of the contented black middle class further, white people (as well as many African Americans) often see middle-class blacks as the antidote for the ills of black America—lifesaving role models who can inspire the less fortunate to transcend their malaise and dispossession. The myth that the problems of the inner city are due to a lack of middle-class role models, however, ignores the well-documented sociological and economic reasons for urban poverty. The effects of urban blight and displacement, of the legacy of slavery and institutionalized racism that decimated millions of black people's lives, and of the still relentless if passive racism that damages black people's sense of security and power: these cause harm that is unlikely to be cured by parading middle-class exemplars before poor people.

The white person's belief that any black person who works hard enough can succeed and subsequently transcend the harsh realities of poverty and racism was made clear by the reaction of white viewers to *The Cosby Show,* the highest-rated situation comedy of the 1980s. In an insightful survey of the program's fans, sociologists Sut Jhally and Justin Lewis reported that many white people felt the series, which portrayed a successful upper-middle-class black family, showed a "world where race no longer matters"—a hopeful view that enabled whites to "combine an impeccably liberal attitude toward race with a deep-rooted suspicion of black people." In other words, Bill Cosby's reassuring portrayal of hardworking, upstanding obstetrician Dr. Cliff Huxtable and his respectable brood did little to dispel the myth that most other, less fortunate black people are bad or lazy or that well-to-do blacks are somehow unfairly benefiting from white benevolence, affirmative action, and quotas. The Huxtable family became white America's model of upper-middle-class black self-sufficiency and transcendence; if only poorer blacks could follow their example!

This opposition between the black underclass and the black middle class tends to leave out the working-class or lower-middle-class people who make up a majority of the black population. Most blacks are no different from their white counterparts in terms of the sacrifices they make to remain economically solvent. Most black men and women work hard to feed and clothe their families and themselves. Their lives are far different from those of the coterie of famous and wealthy black men and women—Cosby, Colin Powell, Oprah Winfrey—whose exalted status in the media triggers admiration and, at the same time, overshadows the real problems and successes of middle-class and working-class blacks.

G A M E S

In ninth grade I dreaded the two Monday-afternoon periods devoted to physical education. All weekend, I would worry about gym. I could hardly eat or sleep. The teacher, Mr. Romeo, was a tall, muscular, stone-faced black man—an ex-Marine who acted more like a drill sergeant than a teacher. I don't know if he pitied me or hated me. My long, spindly arms were not strong enough to hoist me up the ropes, do a dozen push-ups, or propel me gracefully over the pommel horse.

But one Monday afternoon, in front of the class, Mr. Romeo announced that he was confident that my "strong" legs made me a "perfect candidate" to do a "split." He asked me to follow his lead. As my limbs inched away from each other and my crotch lowered perilously close to the floor, I lost my balance. While my classmates laughed and the teacher shook his head in frustration (loudly ordering me to practice the split each day at home), I lay on the cold wood floor humiliated and terrified.

After that, I schemed to get out of gym class. On the suggestion of Mrs. Mosley, I struck a deal with the assistant principal: I would tutor kids in English if he let me out of gym. He agreed. The class would be limited to male students—in this case, five black kids, all of whom I knew and liked. Our classroom would be an airless library storeroom. Before he dismissed me, the assistant principal, who was white, advised me not to be too discouraged by the "low quality" of my students. He knew that I wanted to become a high school teacher and hoped that a bad experience with these students would not dissuade me from my goal. *"Schwartzes,"* he whispered into my ear, with a wink in his eye and an arm around my shoulders, "are poor learners." It took just seven months to reverse the devastating effects of years of this kind of self-fulfilling prophecy, seven months to see my students' enthusiasm for reading blossom, seven months for four of their reading test scores to rise significantly.

SEGREGATION

Rose-Lee Goldberg, a historian and teacher, tells this story:

When I was growing up in a typical liberal Jewish household in South Africa in the 1960s, the relationship between the races was always paradoxical. Although blacks and whites remained apart, we engaged each other in everyday life. My father had a practice in a black area; my mother was a schoolteacher. Our cook was Zulu. My nanny was Xhosa. It was both sad and touching. You actually witnessed exchanges of sweetness and kindness between blacks and whites.

I was aware from my early childhood of what the politics of apartheid was doing to South Africa. I would see blacks running to get home before the eleven o'clock curfew. I was always afraid that the police, who were swinging big clubs above our heads, were going to capture and beat the black people. There wasn't a day that I didn't witness some horrible cruelty against black people.

I lived in a world of racial separation, but as a child, I had this longing, this yearning, for it not to be that way. When I was twelve years old—at the time of the Sharpeville massacre—I made up my mind to get out of there. I wanted to live a life where I could choose my friends. In 1975, after eight years in Europe, I came to the United States. I was in my late twenties. The cultural scene I entered in New York was exclusively white. We never discussed black culture or race; there was a total lack of racial politics.

I would sit on subways and look at black faces (whites and blacks rarely said anything to each other in public situations) and think, "That person must be of Zulu ancestry." Or, "The man across the aisle must be northern African in his ancestry." I came to the United States knowing what African faces looked like. In America, I was shocked that there was no place for whites and blacks to cross over into each other's cultures. There was no place even to make black acquaintances.

Twenty years later, I am intrigued by how separate the races really are in the United States. One group completely doesn't exist for the other. When I was young, my friends and I longed to speak Zulu; we longed to know the other culture. There was a lot of crossing over. It's like Americans can't get beyond the slave complex—slavery cut off black culture from serious white consideration. Yes, there are a couple of pop venues for white appreciation of black culture, but in the end there is no real curiosity.

I tried to teach my children about black culture. I thought I could transcend the impulse to be racist by giving my children a more liberated view of black culture. When I attended my first Martin Luther King Day celebration at my daughter's school, I was shocked to see that the kids were being introduced to black culture only through the story of American racism. My daughter's introduction to black culture in school was really about the oppression of black people. Are we teaching our students about the liberation struggles of blacks, or are we teaching them that black people don't matter unless they are oppressed? When Americans ask me if I'm ashamed to admit that I'm South African, I wonder if they should be ashamed to admit that they are American.

FATHER

One night in the winter of 1960—I was three and a half years old—my father was taken from our Coney Island apartment (where we lived before we moved to the Lower East Side) to a state psychiatric hospital. He would remain there for six months. I do not remember what led up to this. I can only recall the sounds I heard that evening. I lay crying and shaking in my bed, listening to the muffled voices of attendants in the next room strapping him into a straitjacket. I heard my father plead hysterically. I heard him growl at my mother that he would divorce her for committing him to a mental institution. I heard him weep for his mother. I heard the attendants gag his screams. And then I heard nothing.

Although my father was never hospitalized or treated for mental illness again, every February, around the time of his birthday, he would retreat into his own private world. His journeys into insanity always began the same way: he would berate and threaten my mother, my sister, or me for some imagined offense, wait for one of us to defend the other, accuse us all of betraying him, and then descend into a long, stony paranoid silence. Once, when I was fifteen, the process began with my father accusing me of stealing the plastic Bic pen I had borrowed from a store clerk to fill out a form. My father, who watched in silence as I absentmindedly walked out of the art-supply store with the pen in my hand, grabbed me by the arm and forced me to go back inside and apologize for the theft. The muteness that followed such incidents, his refusal to speak—sometimes for as long as six weeks—was brutal and unalterable. Until the spell was broken, there was no way of getting through to him.

My father's hostile silences elicited muteness in kind; it was difficult not to get trapped in a cycle of frustration, emotional withdrawal, and anger that only reinforced his feelings of woundedness and alienation. Each February, I watched helplessly as he imprisoned himself in a metaphorical straitjacket, binding the arms and hands that at most other times demonstrated affection, constricting the chest that at most other times I was allowed to lay my head on, clapping shut the mouth that at most other times spoke words of love and encouragement. During these periods, it was difficult not to hate my father.

Even through my father's worst psychotic episodes, even through his most icy façade, I could make out his weakness, his pain. For most of his life, he had been demoralized: by an insane mother who whipped him and tied him to his bed; by his inability to graduate from college or to achieve his dream of becoming an architect; by the cycle of unemployment, under-employment, and poverty that he could not break; by the schiz-ophrenia that screwed up his relationships and his professional life. When my father was lucid, his extroverted personality and dazzling, analytical intelligence helped to conceal these failures, compromises, and disappointments. During psychotic episodes, when he was unable to suppress his insecurities and self-hatred, they rose vindictively from the unconscious to the surface of his body. His broad shoulders slumped. His head jutted forward. His eyes darkened. His gait became less confident.

My father was born to a Hungarian housewife and a Russian junk dealer in a tenement on the Lower East Side in 1914. With the exception of a few years during World War II, when he worked in Los Angeles and Washington, D.C., as a clerk for the Veterans Administration (because of his severe asthma, he was exempted from military service), he spent his life in the ghetto. The project apartment he died in was a hundred yards from the Lower East Side street where he was born. He had no ambition to transcend this poverty: he would not even entertain my mother's pleas for him to get a better job so we could move to a subsidized apartment in the white, middle-income cooperative buildings on Grand Street nearby. Content with living on unemployment checks or on the meager salary he brought home as an accountant, my father was afraid he would wind up in the hospital if he pushed himself too hard: "Don't rock the boat" was always his answer to my mother's appeals for change.

More than the anti-Semitism that confronted Jewish men of my father's generation, poverty and psychosis played a sig-nificant role in his sense of disfranchisement. It was not that anti-Semitism did not affect my father and his peers—Jewish quotas existed in some universities until after World War II, housing was restricted, and many firms and businesses limited or prohibited the hiring of Jews—but there were professional pathways, in law, in medicine, in education, in business, that preceding generations of Jews had made a bit easier to follow.

My father—who was six feet two inches tall, with pale skin, light-brown hair, and blue eyes, and who psychiatrists later determined had an exceptionally high IQ—needed to do the things that most resourceful sons of Eastern European Jewish immigrants did for success: complete his education in good standing, nurture his talents, make connections within his family and the Jewish community and with professionals in his field. But something held him back. He dropped out of Baruch College at the end of his freshman year. He never reached out to the community. He never read architectural journals.

Insubordinate behavior got him fired from one junior accounting position after another. Constantly belittling his relatives—he regularly called his oldest sister an "ungraded moron" to her face, a reference to the special gradeless report cards issued to marginally retarded students—he grew estranged from his entire family. Even though he was an Orthodox Jew, he took neither solace nor support from organized religion. Each Saturday morning, he would conduct his own Sabbath services in our living room, chanting invocations he either adapted from prayer books and the Old Testament or wrote himself. He stopped attending synagogue in the early 1960s because he felt that the middle-class Jews there resented his poverty. An intensely political and partisan man, he stopped voting in the

late 1960s because he felt that his vote could not make a difference. Even his final illness could not shake his resolve to live a
disaffected and compromised life. With his wife dying and his
own heart failing rapidly, my father refused to move from the
run-down and dangerous project he had lived in for twenty
years to a state-of-the-art low-income apartment building a few
blocks away.

INTEGRATION

During the opening credits of the 1995 movie *Dangerous Minds,* the camera pans across a Hollywood facsimile of a ghetto street. Shot in black and white, the scene suggests film noir mystery and hints of evil. Drug pushers roll down car windows to make their exchanges. Black and Hispanic mothers, cigarettes dangling from their mouths and oversize gold earrings hanging from their ears, ignore their kids. Gang members make their way down filthy streets. When a large bus pulls into view, some of these hapless people slowly, absentmindedly, get on board. And just as the bus pulls away, the film startlingly changes from austere black and white to glistening color as the camera cuts to its destination: an integrated high school at the end of a sunny, tree-lined street. The message is clear: these lucky kids are temporarily leaving behind a degraded, hopeless place for the world of whiteness.

This opening scene, like the rest of the film, reads as a paradigm of integration: poor black and Hispanic people, destined to fail in their own unequal world, will improve their chances by living, learning, and working with their more successful and less oppressed white brothers and sisters. The story line of *Dangerous Minds* pushes this idea to an extreme: a beautiful, white ex-Marine, LouAnne Johnson (played by Michelle Pfeiffer), is hired as a last-minute replacement to teach a special class of smart but socially challenged kids. From her first encounter with these students, we realize the difficulty of her task. As the camera inspects the rambunctious mob of loud rappers, delinquents, and nasty, back-talking girls—"rejects from hell," Johnson calls them later on—we sense that these kids are hopeless. Several teachers before her have quit in frustration, but Johnson gives the job her military best. She devises clever ways of disciplining and finally getting through to her students. She teaches them karate. She rewards them with candy bars. She acknowledges their problems. She makes hair-raising excursions into the inner city to track down their indifferent or ignorant parents.

Her students and their lives, however, are hardly the point of this film. Like most Hollywood movies about racial oppression, *Dangerous Minds* focuses not on the people of color who struggle to survive but on the heroic white person who assumes the task of taming and eventually saving them. Alan Parker's *Mississippi Burning* (1988) made a white FBI agent the hero of the 1960s phase of the civil rights movement, instead of the thousands of protesters and freedom workers who risked their lives; Joel Schumacher's *A Time to Kill* (1996) centers its story of racial justice on the workings of a white, small-town Mississippi lawyer. In these and many other instances, people of color are used as plot devices and props, their lives the backdrop to or catalyst for stories about white valor, selflessness, or benevolence.

This privileging of whiteness extends to the reporting of real events. When Jonathan Levin, a dedicated white high school teacher in the South Bronx, was robbed and murdered in 1997, allegedly by a former student, journalists who covered the story, both in New York and nationally, dwelled on the teacher's decision to work in the ghetto despite the fact that his father, Gerald Levin, was the CEO of Time Warner. In effect, Levin's commitment to his poor black and Hispanic students—a commitment that involved questionable acts of extracurricular generosity, including lending them money, treating them to movies and dinners, and rewarding them with jewelry and other gifts— was raised to the level of saintliness; his very whiteness and wealth rendered him more remarkable than the hundreds of New York City teachers, many of them black and Hispanic people of modest means, who have, sometimes in the face of life-threatening violence, enriched and even saved the lives of their disadvantaged students.

As far back as the U.S. Supreme Court's landmark desegregation rulings in the 1950s, whites edifying blacks has been the subtext of integration. By extolling the virtues of busing, the ultimate integrationist solution, *Dangerous Minds* reiterates this message. The bus that brings these kids into a more reasonable and socially responsible world—a world exemplified not by their parents or the school's black principal, who is portrayed as insensitive and reckless, but by their educated white teachers— becomes the film's metaphor for black salvation. When an angry

African American student asks Ms. Johnson why she, as a white person, does not have to be bused to a better life, she replies that "there are a lot of people who live in your neighborhood who choose not to get on that bus." Johnson continues:

> What do they choose to do? They choose to go out and sell drugs. They choose to go out and kill people. They choose to do a lot of other things. But they choose not to get on that bus. The people who choose to get on that bus, which are you, are the people who are saying: "I will not carry myself down to die, when I go to my grave my head will be high . . ."

The bus becomes Johnson's (and integration's) central metaphor for redemption through association with whiteness. The last quotation is taken from Johnson's lecture on Bob Dylan's "Mr. Tambourine Man." Realizing that her students are too restless to listen to conventional poetry, she turns to popular music—not African American or Latin music but one of *her* white musical heroes. In the twisted multicultural logic of *Dangerous Minds,* where only whiteness has the power to set the world straight, teaching the music of Odetta, Jimi Hendrix, Los Lobos, or Tracy Chapman would be counterproductive.

Later Ms. Johnson fashions a Dylan/Dylan contest in which she asks the students to find a Dylan Thomas poem that is similar to Bob Dylan's "Mr. Tambourine Man." The scene in which the victor claims his prize—dinner with Ms. Johnson at an expensive French restaurant—is the film's most unfortunate set piece. As a pretentious, condescending white waiter, posh accent and all, unctuously describes specials of the day (*confit de canard* and foie gras), the Hispanic teenager stares off into space. He is an updated Eliza Doolittle: a bright but uncivilized kid who, with the right training in white upper-class customs and mores, may be transformed into an acceptable man. Ms. Johnson's benevolent whiteness and the benevolence of integration are the film's main interests. When a student is threatened by a drug pusher, she allows him to take refuge in her house. When he is killed later, she is overwhelmed by her inability to save him and decides to leave the school. Johnson's students, afraid of losing her understanding and generosity, tearfully remind her that she is their "Tambourine Man"—an odd association considering that she had earlier explained to them that "Mr. Tambourine Man" was Bob Dylan's metaphor for a drug pusher.

J E W

(1968)

One afternoon, my sixth-grade public-school teacher asked the class if anyone had a relative in Vietnam. The tallest student in the class, a black kid named James, told us that his brother was in basic training. He was certain that his brother would be sent to Vietnam and that he would die. The teacher, a young white woman, became visibly angry and upset. It is tragic, she told us, that the President of the United States, making life-and-death decisions in a state of isolation and privilege, has condemned so many of our poor and black children to die in a senseless war. James raised his hand. "But President Johnson is Jewish," he said. "Jews don't know what it's like to be poor or black. They don't care about us."

(1968)

My mother held up black anti-Semitism as further evidence of black people's unworthiness. The bitter New York City teachers' strike of 1968—a strike that drove a wedge between parents demanding greater control of a public-school system increasingly populated by black and Hispanic students and a teachers' union whose membership was mostly white and Jewish—gave my mother powerful ammunition. The union, content with the status quo and quick to reject plans by New York City and New York State to decentralize the school system in order to give parents a greater voice in their children's education, voted overwhelmingly to strike. A number of black parents and their advocates responded with anti-Semitic epithets. The ensuing hostilities provoked Jewish racism and black anti-Semitism as they shattered the strong political bond between two groups formerly allied in the civil rights movement. My mother used the anti-Jewish rhetoric as a club with which she tried to pressure her husband and children into believing that blacks were bad. People who called us "devils" had to be bad. People who called us "bloodsuckers" had to be bad. People who called us "greedy Jews" had to be bad.

(1969)

A great topic of conversation among New York Jews, including my mother and father, was the controversial *Harlem on My Mind* exhibition at the Metropolitan Museum of Art. The show, curated by the cultural historian Allon Schoener, himself a Jew, was one of the first art museum exhibitions to showcase contemporary black American life through photographs, sound recordings, and text. Many politicians and cultural figures viewed the show as anti-Semitic. It was actually the introductory essay in the show's catalogue—originally a term paper written by Candice Van Ellison, a seventeen-year-old black student at Theodore Roosevelt High School in the Bronx—that was thought to be anti-Semitic, or, more specifically, a paradigm of black anti-Jewish sentiment. This passage, reprinted in the newspapers, was often cited as evidence that black parents were nurturing hatred of Jews in their sons and daughters:

> Anti-Jewish feeling is a natural result of the black Northern migration. Afro-Americans in Northeastern industrial cities are constantly coming in contact with Jews. Pouring into lower-income areas in the city, the Afro-American pushes out the Jew. Behind every hurdle that the Afro-American has yet to jump stands the Jew who has already cleared it . . . Thus, our contempt for the Jew makes us feel more completely American in sharing a national prejudice.

[1971]

In junior high school, I attended a special PTA meeting on budget cuts. As I walked into the school auditorium, I could sense the kind of toxic anticipation that was in the air whenever black and Hispanic parents were about to face the white faculty and staff members. The hostile atmosphere demoralized me. I was proud of the fact that many of my black and Hispanic classmates had become my friends. The meeting, however, disabused me of the notion that this goodwill extended much beyond the circumstances of my odd life. The death of this fantasy came in an ugly, nauseating flash: the instant it took the black PTA president to dig her long, red-painted nails into the forearm of the white assistant principal (the same obnoxious man who had earlier warned me that *schwartzes* were "poor learners") and announce that it was "too bad" Hitler hadn't "gotten" every last Jew on earth.

R A C E

Paul Caruso, a college student and manager of the communications center of a major business magazine, tells these stories:

I grew up in a mostly white section of Park Slope, Brooklyn. My dad worked for Con Edison, the gas and electric company, for forty-three years. My mom worked most of her life as an accountant. My dad was from Sicily; my mom was from Naples. They had a strong, middle-class work ethic. They raised five children. I went to a Catholic grammar school and later to a Catholic high school. Racism was never a factor in my life. I was surrounded by such a diverse group of people. I was involved in after-school programs where I played with black kids. I don't know why racism was never a factor. Maybe it was our upbringing. We were just there to have a good time and play.

My first personal experience with racism came when I was eight years old. I was a juvenile diabetic. I used to go to Camp NYDA in the summers—the camp of the New York Diabetes Association. Seven of the other children in my bunk were white; two were black. For whatever reason, one of the black kids did not get along with me. I tried to be friends with him and it just didn't happen. Things got worse. At one point, we went outside the bunk and had a big fistfight. We fought hard. The seven white kids were cheering me on. The other black kid was obviously rooting for the black kid. That's when I opened my eyes and realized—I was all of eight years old—that the way the kids divided up was about race and nothing else.

A lot of my friends are racist. I had friends in high school who did not like black people. I had friends who just stuck with their own kind. Most of them were Irish or Italian, and they did not like blacks or Jews. They used racial slurs like "nigger," "black piece of shit," "fucking niggers." I probably heard these words when I was younger, but I wasn't affected by them. As I got older, I realized what was going on around me. And then these words began to sink in. But mind you, some of *my* best friends in high school were black. I still keep in touch with some of them to this day.

College has been difficult for me financially. I have never really been able to afford my tuition. I always supported myself. I am putting myself through college. When I first started Kingsborough Community College, I was working in a gourmet shop, not making very much money. I applied for financial aid, and my application was denied. The government said I made too much money. That was a real kick in the ass. I was struggling, barely able to support myself, and I couldn't get any tuition assistance.

I felt cheated. All the financial aid went to black people. They got the aid because of their color and their background. The fact that they weren't working enabled them to get unemployment, food stamps, and free tuition. They had a free ticket to life. I was insulted. I was angry. I was frustrated. Bad things were going on in my mind. I felt hatred. I was sour. I was mad at the black students for not having to pay tuition. I was mad at the government and the school. I was mad at myself for even working. I took it hard.

I still have a problem with all of this. I think that affirmative action programs and preferential treatment both help and hurt. Minority groups are in need of help in certain situations, and I'm all for that. I think these programs hurt because they enable minorities to do nothing, to some extent. They give minorities the easy way out. I have no problem with helping minorities, unless it's like the situation I had. Then there will be some tension. There is a fine line with equal opportunity. What is equal? What's equal to you may not be equal to me.

H A I R [2]

My parents seldom gave my sister and me presents, not even for our birthdays. Sometimes my father would spontaneously give me things he found at the odd-lot discount shop near where he worked in downtown Manhattan: a stethoscope, a gyroscope, a collection of igneous rocks. I can recall only one present from my mother—the hairbrush, comb, and tube of Alberto VO5 hair cream she gave me for my fifteenth birthday. By then my hair, which had been straight and blond when I was a child, had grown thick, dark, and curly. She hated the "natural" look. She demanded no less from her "handsome" son than a "neat and well-groomed" head of hair. My high school yearbook picture records in perpetuity the fruit of my mother's efforts: a shock of frizzy, glistening, gently suppressed waves divided off to one side by a crisp part.

T R U S T

Alvin Hall, a financial-services training professional, tells this story:

Six years ago, I founded a business that designs custom training programs and exam preparation courses for Wall Street firms. Wall Street, no matter what anyone says, is still not very integrated. People respond to me in the financial markets as a black person. And as a black teacher on Wall Street, I've encountered situations where people have judged me to be unqualified to teach because I was black.

In one of the oldest firms, for example, I had a particularly distressing experience. Even though my evaluations were excellent and many students considered me the best teacher in the company, I knew I had to be perfect in order to survive. I *was* perfect. My grammar was perfect. My clothes were perfect. My delivery was perfect. My grooming was perfect. I knew that when students first saw my black face I had a brief window of opportunity to convince them that I was worth listening to. I had to be "Mr. Perfection" in order for them to trust me.

Only after this initial period of trust building would I work black references into my lecture: I would quote Aretha Franklin songs, or use the word "ain't" or double negatives. Gradually my students would become more comfortable with my world. But first I had to start out being essentially a black person who looks like white people, wants what white people want, needs what white people need, and speaks in a language that white people can hear.

What I have come to learn in the financial world is that white people really want black people to act "white," and being the black Alvin Hall was becoming a problem for me. The more this particular class was responding to my style, the more the white training director became combative. He eventually insisted that I be removed from class. He said I was using "inappropriate" language. He was so incredibly threatened that I have not been allowed to work at that company since.

No matter how integrated their communities, white people have a fairly limited threshold for blackness. Even before I start a class, I must decide whether or not I need to come across as smart *or* successful. Only rarely can I be both at the same time. Sometimes white people are more comfortable with a black person who is smart and struggling than with one who is smart and flourishing. The latter combination can be frightening to them.

To survive in an "integrated" world, black people must always find ways of reinventing themselves in order to make sure that white people are comfortable with them. In the course of an all-day class with new students, I often metamorphose into six or seven different people to calm their fears and insecurities: the perfect, unthreatening 1950s Negro, like Sidney Poitier in *Lilies of the Field;* the suave 1960s black matinee idol; the 1950s homemaker, the June Cleaver type who reassures my older, white male students that they are smart and in command; the Eddie Murphy character, who piques their curiosity and perks them up with jokes. If I sense that my white students are relaxing, I can inject more of myself into the lecture. If they are uptight, I'll have to cycle through these personae, tailoring them as I go along. I want my students to reach a comfort level that allows them to accept the knowledge that I can offer them. If I was totally Alvin Hall—Alvin Hall as black man—they would not want to learn from me. I'm sure that many of them think I go home and listen to opera at night. Little do they know that I listen to rap music, too.

CAUGHT

Outside of my years in the Hebrew day school, I wasn't used to being around white kids. The first time I walked into the lunchroom of the Fiorello H. La Guardia High School of Music and Art, a specialized school for gifted teenagers, I became paralyzed with confusion. In the middle of Harlem, on the campus of City College, where the school was then located, the cafeteria was like something out of Jim Crow America with an imaginary line drawn down its center. White and Asian American students had gravitated to one side; black and Hispanic students to the other.

On the first day of school, I befriended Kevin Nelson, a black kid in my homeroom who, like me, lived in a low-income housing project. I knew only that I wanted to sit with him. Yet I did not know where I belonged. My first instinct, my primal instinct, was to sit with the white students in whose faces I saw my own whiteness reflected. I was also afraid to sit with the black and Hispanic students, because I did not know what they would think or say if I invaded "their" turf.

Kevin and I decided we would try the white side of the lunchroom. As we made ourselves comfortable, sitting next to a dark-skinned Jewish girl and an equally swarthy Arab American girl who clearly saw themselves as white, the Arab American student quietly whispered to us that we had to move because we didn't belong there. I ended up retreating with my friend to the black and Hispanic side of the lunchroom, where we ate together for the rest of the school year.

C A I N

If you look, for example, at male monkeys, especially in the wild, roughly half of them survive to adulthood. The other half die by violence. That is the natural way of it for males, to knock each other off, and, in fact, there are some interesting evolutionary implications of that because the same hyper-aggressive monkeys who kill each other are also hypersexual, so they copulate more . . . Maybe it isn't just the careless use of the word when people call certain cities "jungles." *

▪

[African Americans] were jolted into the realization that they, like Rodney King, could be halted by the police, brutalized, kicked, and

---

* Dr. Frederick K. Goodwin, director, Alcohol Drug Abuse and Mental Health Administration (1992), as quoted by Farai Chideya, in *Don't Believe the Hype: Fighting Cultural Misinformation about African-Americans* (1995).

possibly killed, and that their assailants in police uniforms would probably walk away free. They were awakened by the haunting fear that their college-bound sons and daughters could be stopped for minor traffic violations, and later be found dead or lying in the city streets. This is what Representative Floyd Flake of Queens [New York] meant when he explained why the hopes of millions of African-Americans in the inherent fairness of the American legal system were shattered: "when Rodney King was on the ground getting beat, we were all on the ground getting beat." *

Faune, a participant in an Internet conference on race and American culture, posts this story:

A couple of years ago, I was working in a community-based agency in Brooklyn doing adult ed. The administration was all white women. There were a number of people of color among the teaching staff, black and Asian. One day we had a staff-development workshop on, among other things, [ethnic] identity. A white colleague of mine was asked what she thought of her race when she was walking down the street. Her comment (a Freudian slip, I pray and presume) was that she saw it as "superlative." I take it she meant "superfluous."

No black person is EVER unaware of his or her race. Because WHITE society makes that impossible. Regardless of how old I am, or how I'm dressed, or what neighborhood I'm in, women clutch their purses at my approach.

* Manning Marable, *Beyond Black and White* (1995).

I work in a midtown office building where virtually ALL the black folk are in some kind of uniform: security guard, food service, mail-room clerks in smocks. In the ten months I've been there, I have seen fewer than a dozen black people in mufti. After ten months, I still get stares in the corridor.

For no reason other than that I am there.

In America, in New York City, I am still a rarity in an advertising agency.

Now you expect me to believe that white people in [this conference] are appreciably different from those that I see on the street, at work, at school? These are people who don't know any black people and don't care to.

One of the things I like about this conference and others is that people have started to ask and even discuss the harder questions.

But nothing is going to change so long as white people feel they can evade the real issues with tangents about class and blithe proclamations about how *they're* certainly not racist and "why do we have to talk about interrogating whiteness? It's so uncomfortable."

You don't know uncomfortable.

Uncomfortable is walking down the street wearing the mark of Cain for the sin of being the wrong color.

A R T I F A C T

*What is often called the black soul is a white man's artifact.**

■

They were the people who went in for Negroes—Michael and Anne—the Carraways. But not in the social service, philanthropic sort of way, no. They saw no use in helping a race that was already too charming and naïve and lovely for words. Leave them unspoiled and just enjoy them, Michael and Anne felt. So they went in for the Art of Negroes—the dancing that had such jungle life about it, the songs that were so simple and fervent, the poetry that was so direct, so real. They never tried to influence the art, they only bought it and raved over it, and copied it. For they were artists, too.†

---

*   Frantz Fanon, *Black Skin, White Masks* (1952).
†   Langston Hughes, *The Ways of White Folks* (1934).

How one is seen (as black) and, therefore, what one sees (in a white world) is always already critical to one's existence as an Afro-American. The very markers that reveal you to the rest of the world, your dark skin and your kinky/curly hair, are visual. However, not being seen by those who don't want to see you because they are racist, what Ralph Ellison called "invisibility," often leads to the racist interpretation that you are unable *to see. This has meant, among other things, that Afro-Americans have not produced . . . a tradition in the visual arts as vital and compelling to other Americans as the Afro-American tradition in music. Moreover, the necessity . . . for drawing parallels or alignments between Afro-American music and everything else cultural among Afro-Americans, stifles and represses most of the potential for understanding the visual in Afro-American culture.**

This is the history of slavery and conquest, written, seen, drawn, and photographed by The Winners. They cannot be read and made sense of from any other position. The "white eye" is always outside the frame— but seeing and positioning everything within it.†

---

* Michele Wallace, "Modernism, Postmodernism and the Problem of the Visual in Afro-American Culture," in *Out There: Marginalization and Contemporary Cultures* (1990).
† Stuart Hall, "The Whites of Their Eyes: Racial Ideologies and the Media," in *Media Reader* (1990).

ARTIFACT

*The colorless multi-coloredness of whiteness secures white power by making it hard, especially for white people and their media, to "see" whiteness . . . It is the way that black people are marked as black (are not just "people") . . . that has made it relatively easy to analyze their representation, whereas white people—not there as a category and everywhere everything as a fact—are difficult, if not impossible, to analyze qua white. The subject seems to fall apart in your hands as soon as you begin. Any instance of white representation is always immediately something more specific—*Brief Encounter *is not about white people, it is about English middle-class people;* The Godfather *is not about white people, it is about Italian-American people; but* The Color Purple *is about black people, before it is about poor, southern U.S. people.**

---

*   Richard Dyer, "White" (*Screen,* Autumn 1988).

M I R R O R

Kevin Nelson and I were riding home on the subway from high school one afternoon, talking about *All in the Family.* The sitcom, which centers on the exploits of the bigoted loudmouth Archie Bunker and his family and neighbors in a working-class neighborhood in Queens, had its controversial premiere just a few weeks before.

"I really like the way Bunker spews all this racist crap," Kevin began. "It's about time someone on TV talked the way white people *really* talk."

I had already had this discussion before, with my father (who agreed with me). "I can't see how using words like 'coon' and 'kike' is a good thing," I said to Kevin now. "People just love Archie. They think his racism's cool. He makes it even more okay to use the very words that white people use in private all the time. Why is that good?"

"I'd rather see racism out in the open than buried under all the bullshit that says you white people really love black people and that you'd never think of calling us 'nigger,'" Kevin shot back.

His reference to "you white people" made me uncomfortable. I wondered if he really trusted me. I wondered if he knew that I heard the word *schwartze* every day, and from the person I loved most. "I don't know what you're talking about" was all I could muster.

Just as Kevin began to change the subject, a middle-aged black woman tapped me on the shoulder. "Let me tell you something, young man," she said. "White people really hate it when their racism is thrown back in their faces. White people can be so ugly and stupid. You're not worried about *All in the Family* making racism acceptable. What really worries you is that Archie's racism might look a whole lot like your own."

Her comment confused me. It embarrassed me. It made me want to tell her that I wasn't a bigot. Instead, I said nothing, relieved that my best friend was as reluctant as I to take this conversation any further.

C L A S S [2]

At first I did not know what I wanted. But in the end I understood this language. I understood it, I understood it, I understood it, all wrong perhaps. That is not what matters . . . Does this mean that I am freer now than I was? I do not know. I shall learn.

—Samuel Beckett, *Molloy*

My first year of high school was difficult: I was no longer assured of being at the top of my class. According to my teachers and counselors, I didn't even come close. My grade point average was no better than a B+. I avoided discussing where I lived for fear of further alienating the middle- and upper-middle-class white students. In the hierarchy of power that existed at the High School of Music and Art, most of the school's wealthiest (and most successful) students were white. These students, a minority of the student population, lived in some of the most affluent neighborhoods in New York City: the Upper West Side, Park Avenue, Riverdale, Forest Hills. Most of their parents were white-collar professionals and workers—doctors, lawyers, teachers, and businessmen. The school's predominantly white faculty held out its greatest expectations for them. They won many of the awards and commendations.

They were the salutatorian and valedictorian at graduation. They were featured in school exhibitions and recitals. I did not feel particularly connected to these students. As the diverse student population slowly edged toward integration in my second year—with students of color and white students sitting *adjacent* to each other in the lunchroom—I continued to eat with a group of black students.

It was not until my senior year that things began to change. I had always loved to write and had always been a good English student. The English department faculty offered me a coveted seat in the college-level advanced-placement class in twentieth-century literature. The course's gifted instructor was a white man with a Ph.D. in English. I was challenged and intellectually stimulated by both the teacher and the complex readings he assigned: *Death on the Installment Plan, Molloy, Waiting for Godot, A Passage to India, A Streetcar Named Desire.* A tall, handsome man in his late thirties, he made no secret of his homosexuality, and he knew that I too was gay. He insisted that I read *Maurice* for more than just the coincidence of a shared name. The more he praised my efforts, the more I felt I mattered intellectually. By setting an example, he helped me to emerge as a scholar and a gay man.

My outstanding performance in advanced-placement English did not go unnoticed by the school's top students. They even rewarded me with the vice presidency of the school's chapter of Arista, the national high school honor society. I had been accepted, in a sense, into the intellectual elite of the school. Each day at noon, I joined a "club" of four other white advanced-placement English students; we spent our lunch hour eating sandwiches and analyzing some of the more difficult writers of the twentieth century with adolescent passion. For the first time in high school, I was reaching out to the white kids. For the first time in high school, I no longer relied solely on my black and Hispanic peers for friendship.

MYTH

In *Mythologies,* a study of contemporary myth, Roland Barthes wrote about a chance encounter with the image of a black youth in the racially charged Paris of the late 1950s. While waiting at a barbershop for a haircut, Barthes was offered a copy of *Paris-Match.* On the cover was a photograph of an Afro-French child dressed in the uniform of the French military. His hand is raised in salute. His uplifted eyes are fixed in the distance, presumably on the tricolor, that great symbol of French militarism and civility.

The image intrigued Barthes. Writing about it a few years later, he sensed hidden meanings just below its slick surface. He speculated on the magazine editor's motives. He analyzed the ways in which the complex image suggested multiple, even contradictory meanings. Beyond the literal representation of a black soldier boy giving the French salute, the cover suggested to

Barthes another, more manipulative political message: "that France is a great Empire, that all her sons, without any color discrimination, faithfully serve under her flag, and that there is no better answer to the detractors of an alleged colonialism than the zeal shown by this Negro in serving his so-called oppressors." It is this purer (though actually sinister) level of meaning that Barthes identified as myth.

Barthes argued that contemporary myths play a central role in our media-rich society: they conceal the undesirable, make bearable the unbearable, and whitewash the contradictions and dissonances that threaten to disrupt social order. They are a "virus" that infects our reasoning and our politics. These contemporary myths, he concluded, serve "not to deny things" but to take the troubling images in our everyday lives—depictions resonant with our fears, our intolerance, our bigotry—and make "them innocent . . . give . . . them a natural and eternal justification." The myth of the *Paris-Match* cover—that colonialism and racism were no longer problems for the French people—existed to assuage anxiety and guilt at a time when that nation was coming to terms with its own history of brutal racism and colonialism.

Forty years after Barthes directed his uncompromising eye toward society's myths, such deceptions continue to operate. Despite the visual sophistication and supposed vigilance of a media-oriented culture that hits us daily with political exposés and instant polling results, the vast majority of Western commentators, critics, and academics seem not to realize how duplicitous words and images can be. They simply do not understand or do not wish to understand how myths work, how myths hold us hostage to their smooth, elegant fictions.

The subject of race, perhaps more than any other subject in contemporary life, feeds on myth. Myth is the sinister adjective of the white supremacist, delineating a whiteness that is superior, moral, wholesome, stable, intelligent, and talented and a blackness that is inferior, stupid, shiftless, lazy, dishonest, untrustworthy, licentious, and violent. Myth is the cool, seamless narrative that tells us the contradictioins and incongruities of race and racism are too confusing or too dangerous to articulate. Myths provide the elegant deceptions that reinforce our unconscious prejudices. Myths are the white lies that tell us everything is all right, even when it is not.

H Y P E

Hype is myth's media-savvy brother. The newspaper and television reporter, the magazine article, the talk-show interview thrive on hype. Racism and hype are bound up together: racism is built on hype, which in turn is built on stereotype. Blackness and whiteness, filtered through hype, segregate into two opposing, simplistic values. Hype predisposes white people to see even the most innocent black person as dangerous, sinister, or scary: the black medical student walking down a dark street at night *reads* as savage, licentious, criminal. The black mother pushing her son in a stroller down that same street in the light of day *reads* as unmarried and irresponsible.

Racist hype justifies white anxieties about an unknown or unfamiliar blackness. It shores up white power by justifying white people's need to curb black power or expression. These are some of the reasons why it is so hard for white people to acknowledge the lies and distortions that underwrite hype. African American writers and intellectuals, of course, have long challenged racist hype as a means of survival. In *Don't Believe the Hype: Fighting Cultural Misinformation about African-Americans,* the journalist Farai Chideya, an African American woman, combs through a catalogue of ingrained white lies. Chideya fights hype with a reality, as she calls it, gleaned from government surveys, scientific data, interviews, public-opinion polls, and clinical observations.

Nowhere is her book more powerful and challenging of these lies than in the remarkable introductory reader quiz: "Test Your Racial Issues IQ." The test, in the form of multiple-choice questions about the reader's perception of race, is an exercise in self-evaluation. Like a home HIV test, where blood is let in one's own bathroom and sent off to be evaluated anonymously, Chideya's exam reveals its troubling results discreetly. No one but the reader need know how he or she did. (The answers are provided at the end of the quiz.) At its core is an irony of sorts: while racist hype displays its myths in public, the honest and potentially embarrassing inquiry into how it affects the individual is usually possible only in private:

Question #5: Between 1980 and 1990, in terms of the rate of increase for children born to single mothers:
A. The black rate grew nine times as much as the white rate
B. The white rate grew nine times as much as the black rate
C. Both rates are increasing rapidly

D. The black rate is increasing and the white rate is decreasing*

Chideya finds that cultural disinformation about African Americans is everywhere in the media, concerning every aspect of life: sex, love, family values, primary and secondary education, affirmative action, wages and employment patterns, the arts, sports, the criminal justice system, politics. Such media-driven hype continually shapes our thinking about race. No matter how free of racism white people think they are, no matter how much white people love jazz or enjoy the company of black friends, their racial politics cannot help but be distorted by hype. Take one of Chideya's test cases—an analysis of a statement made by Boston University president John Silber, a candidate in the 1990 Massachusetts Democratic gubernatorial primary. When asked during a debate why he did not take his "get tough on crime" message to black neighborhoods, Silber responded: "There is no point in my making a speech on crime control to a bunch of addicts." Rather than questioning his statement, *The Christian Science Monitor,* for example, praised him as "tough talking" and "forthright." Such lack of journalistic rigor, Chideya argues, readily transformed Silber's mythic utterance—that inner-city blacks are addicted to drugs—into a particularly destructive form of hype.

Chideya's questioning of Silber's assertion does what the media would not do: it deflates his racist hype with hard facts and figures. While she acknowledges that drug use tends to be

* Answer: B.

higher in the inner cities than in wealthier neighborhoods, she points out that African Americans, statistically, account for just 12 percent of users—a figure roughly in proportion to black representation in the general population—while more than 70 percent of drug users are white. Yet the association between blackness and drug addiction is perpetuated by a media that continually targets crime committed by urban, African American drug users. In reality, surveys of drug use suggest that African Americans under the age of thirty-five are significantly less likely to have ever used an illegal drug than whites of the same age; among all age groups, 38 percent of whites and 39 percent of blacks say they have used illegal drugs.

Thus, the white communities to which Silber delivered his tough anticrime message sheltered just as many "addicts" as the "hopeless" black enclaves that he shunned. This idea, however, would have been useless to Silber, undermining, as it would have, the subliminal, manipulative rhetoric of his race-baiting campaign.

PASSING

The desire for invisibility, the desire to become "white," lies at the center of the Jew's flight from his or her own body.

—Sander Gilman, *The Jew's Body* (1991)

My mother was driven to create for herself an idealized whiteness, a rigid, carefully measured whiteness she could always count on, a whiteness which would ensure that she would not be mistaken for the black or Hispanic denizens of the projects she hated so much. Her beauty rituals culminated in a façade, not the usual thick veil of makeup favored by women of her generation but a mask that would allow her to enter the world each day a "respectable" light-skinned white woman.

Like so many immigrants of her generation who could not tolerate or did not want to suffer the consequences of having dark skin, or like the generations of light-skinned African American people who have masqueraded as white in an effort to survive or succeed in a world that despises or distrusts their blackness, my mother was passing. And like any person who chooses to pass, it was discrimination—real and anticipated—that drove her to paint on the mask of a purer whiteness.

On one level, the weirdness of my mother's masquerade isolated her. It kept away the black and Hispanic neighbors, whom she loathed, and the white Jews who shopped in her favorite supermarkets and whom she openly castigated but secretly envied because they were not dark and because they were not poor. The mask she wore every day made her look strange and uninviting. She didn't look whiter—she looked like a person who was concealing something under layers of greasepaint. She rarely talked to anyone. She rarely looked at anyone. Her face became a blank screen onto which she could project a range of character types: the stately, elegant lady who was too good for the projects; the cultivated, charming matron who would later accompany her son, the art historian, to the museum, not to look at art but to be around other "affluent" white people; the WASP bitch who would not even look her neighbors in the eye.

Her behavior has always been a kind of mystery to me. What exactly were the rewards for turning her face, layer upon layer, morning after morning, into a mask of pure whiteness?

P A S S I N G [2]

Let me tell you how I'd get those white devil convicts and the guards,
too, to do anything I wanted. I'd whisper to them, "If you don't, I'll
start a rumor that you're really a light Negro just passing as white."
That shows you what the white devil thinks about the black man. He'd
*rather die than be thought a Negro.**

We all ordered fish and settled down comfortably to shocking our white
friends with tales about how many Negroes there were passing for white
all over America. We were determined to épater le bourgeois *real good*
via this white couple we had cornered, when the woman leaned over the
table in the midst of our dissertation and said, "Listen, gentlemen, you

---

* Malcolm X, *The Autobiography of Malcolm X* (1965).

needn't spread the word, but me and my husband aren't white either. We've just been passing for white for the last fifteen years."

"What?"

*"We're colored, too, just like you," said the husband. "But it's better passing for white because we make more money."**

■

She said: "It's funny about 'passing.' We disapprove of it and at the same time condone it. It excites our contempt and yet we rather admire it. We shy away from it with an odd kind of revulsion, but we protect it."

"Instinct of the race to survive and expand."

"Rot! Everything can't be explained by some general biological phrase."

"Absolutely everything can. Look at the so-called whites, who've left bastards all over the known earth. Same thing in them. Instinct of the race to survive and expand."†

■

She quietly went about her clerical tasks, not once revealing her true identity. She listened to the women with whom she worked discuss their worries—their children's illnesses, their husband's disappointments, their boyfriends' infidelities—all of the mundane yet critical things that made up their lives. She came to know them but they did not know her,

---

* Langston Hughes, "Who's Passing for Who?" (*Negro Story*, December 1945/ January 1946).
† Nella Larsen, *Passing* (1929).

for my grandmother occupied a completely different place. That place—where white supremacy and economic domination meet—was unknown turf to her white co-workers. They remained oblivious to the worlds within worlds that existed just beyond the edge of their awareness and yet were present in their very midst.

Every evening, my grandmother, tired and worn, retraced her steps home, laid aside her mask, and reentered herself. Day in and day out, she made herself invisible, then visible again, for a price too inconsequential to do more than barely sustain her family and at a cost too precious to conceive.*

---

*   Cheryl I. Harris, "Whiteness as Property," in *Critical Race Theory: The Key Writings That Formed the Movement* (1995).

P R O J E C T I O N

Like many liberal Jews in the 1950s and 1960s, my father saw blackness as an extension of his own Jewishness—a similar disfranchisement. He projected his own fears of being beaten down onto the civil rights struggles of black Americans. Blackness, for him, was synonymous with all of the different ways he thought he was (and actually was) disconnected from the powerful, white, Christian, complacent mainstream. Blackness, in *his* mind, came to represent Jewishness, poverty, unemployment, mental illness. Racism against black people was of a piece with all the prejudices, perceived and real, that had victimized him: hatred of Jews, hatred of poor people, hatred of the mentally ill.

In the course of rethinking the meaning of victimhood and alienation in my father's life, I have come to see some flaws in his generally admirable racial politics. It is easy for me to recall the wonderful things he said about race and black people. From the time I was eight or nine, we usually spent Friday nights talking about American politics. Our hushed conversations, illuminated by the flickering light of the Sabbath candles, were filled with his insights and beneficence about race in America: his passionate support of black leaders such as Martin Luther King, Medgar Evers, Ralph Bunche, A. Philip Randolph, Thurgood Marshall, and Bayard Rustin; his adoration of black singers and actors such as Paul Robeson, Cab Calloway, Ossie Davis and Ruby Dee, Harry Belafonte, and Sidney Poitier; his efforts to teach me about the history of slavery and emancipation; his staunch defense of Harlem Representative Adam Clayton Powell, Jr., after he was expelled from Congress for "misuse of public funds" (he saw Powell's martyrdom as the inevitable power play of white congressmen who resented his seniority and clout); his hatred of white racists such as George Wallace, William Shockley, George Lincoln Rockwell, and Orval Faubus; his abhorrence of capital punishment (he believed, correctly as it turned out, that the death penalty was disproportionately applied to black criminals); his defiance of my mother in warning me never to use the words *schwartze,* nigger, or Negro when referring to black people.

Back then I was in awe of my father's knowledge and his compassion and fairness. Now I find myself a bit troubled by this thinking, concerned that all too often he viewed blackness through the lens of his own victimhood rather than through the individual strengths, weaknesses, and humanity of black people. A loner, my father had no black friends or acquaintances, even though most of his neighbors were black. He made no effort to know these people. Blackness was what he read about in the papers, saw on television, or incidentally observed or encountered on the street or the subway. Blackness was, for him, the ultimate ideal and the ultimate form of transcendence. Black heroes—and he had many—were untouchable; they were to be adored for their sanctity and worshipped for the ways in which they overcame adversity.

Just as my mother struggled to obliterate her darkness, my father projected himself into blackness. He loved black people who survived what seemed the same bigotry that was crippling him. I think he would have liked to pass for black himself. But he could not. His blue eyes and pale skin would not have permitted it. The fact that society marked him as white from the day he was born would not have permitted it. His fear of black people's ridicule and rejection would not have permitted it.

ARETHA

All through my childhood and into my teens, I remained caught in racial limbo, trapped between my identification with blackness and the awareness that I would never be anything but white. The pull of the two worlds was great: a racist mother and an antiracist father; an Orthodox Jewish life inside the home and a life outside infused with Christianity and blackness; teachers who believed that only the culture of white people mattered and others who taught me about civil rights and the accomplishments of black people. On Saturday mornings, I would awaken to the sounds of two different worlds: the muffled baritone of my father chanting Hebrew prayers coming through my bedroom door, and the Motown records—Aretha Franklin, Marvin Gaye, the Supremes, the Jackson Five—blaring through my windows.

Aretha I secretly loved. In the fifth grade—it was 1967—I would sneak into the auditorium after school to watch a group of black girls rehearse for the monthly talent show. I looked on in awe as they "played" Aretha, bobbing their heads back and forth, waving their hands elegantly in the air, lip-synching the words to "Respect" and "Think." I wanted to play Aretha, too. I wanted to be hip and cool like Aretha, like these girls. I never told my mother how I felt, but I think she knew. Every time Aretha would appear on *The Ed Sullivan Show,* my eyes would fix on the screen and I would lean forward. My mother would rush over to the television set and turn off the sound, because Aretha was a "screamer," not a singer, not someone she or her children needed to hear. I kept on staring into the singer's broad, animated face, discreetly rocked my head back and forth, and mouthed the soulful lyrics that my mother feared might come between us.

M E M O R Y

From the past, it is my childhood which fascinates me most; these images alone, upon inspection, fail to make me regret the time which has vanished. For it is not the irreversible I discover in my childhood, it is the irreducible: everything which is still in me, by fits and starts; in the child, I read quite openly the dark underside of myself.*

■

The deepest shame often accompanies our will not to remember—shame which is not fleeting although we often treat memory that way, as though being revisionists of our own past made much of a difference, as in, "Actually I believe my childhood to have been quite happy. We had a dog, a psychiatrist, a house and what not," and so forth . . . To be

---

* Roland Barthes, *Roland Barthes* (1975).

central and apparently loved, one will do a great deal, even exercise, con-
tinually, the courage of shutting up, the conviction that yes I am just like
you and everyone else or at least exhibit the desire to be. At home, in the
face of the parent, self-censorship [looms] as the entry fee into the ruined
*kingdom of their existence, of lies and lies again . . . ***

My job becomes how to rip that veil drawn over "proceedings too terrible
to relate." The exercise is also critical for any person who is black, or
who belongs to any marginalized category, for historically, we were sel-
dom invited to participate in the discourse even when we were its topic.
Moving that veil aside requires certain things. First of all, I must trust
my own recollections. I must also depend on the recollections of others.
Thus memory weighs heavily in what I write, in how I begin and in
what I find to be significant. Zora Neale Hurston said, "Like the dead-
seeming cold rocks, I have memories within that came out of the material
that went to make me." These "memories within" are the subsoil of my
work.†

---

* Hilton Als, "It Will Soon Be Here," in *Critical Fictions: The Politics of Imaginative Writing* (1991).
† Toni Morrison, "The Site of Memory," in *Inventing the Truth: The Art and Craft of Memoir* (1987).

BROTHER

The only black person who ever disappointed my father was Malcolm X. What turned my father against Malcolm X was not his Black Muslim creed (which many Jews perceived as anti-Semitic and anti-Zionist) but his advocacy of a politics of exclusion and black nationalism. There was no place in Malcolm X's separatist worldview for my father, or for any other white person who saw himself as a fellow traveler. And even though Malcolm X began to move away from this strident separatism in the last years of his life, his change of heart was too late for my father, who had been too wounded by the black leader's words even to notice. To be pushed away by a black man, by a potential surrogate for his own pain and disfranchisement, felt like the ultimate betrayal.

S K I N

Maria Phillips, an anthropology student, tells this story:

I was working for a small advertising company whose client roster included large corporations, small businesses, and public-service organizations. The company often accepted, and even sought, projects that addressed social problems such as AIDS awareness and racial and economic discrimination. While the company's directors may have been well intentioned, their decision-making processes in some instances revealed deeply held beliefs that not only affirmed certain stereotypes but sometimes produced work that perpetuated the very evils the company sought to attack.

One event provides an example of good intentions gone bad. A human rights organization solicited design firms internationally to create posters that would protest the history of "global oppression" of minority peoples. The company I worked for came up with a concept meant to produce a powerful, visceral response—one that would stimulate a viewer's righteous indignation against racism. Once an overall design had been chosen, test shots were to be made for the poster's central image—a head shot of a downtrodden, oppressed black person. Since I was the only black person working in the office, I was asked to sit for a photograph. Initially, I was amused that I was asked, because I often functioned in similar ways as the resident person of color. But my amusement was short-lived. The next day, I experienced the all-too-familiar creepiness of condescending racial apologies. I was pulled aside and told, very carefully, that my photo had been rejected for the final poster, because, well, I didn't look "black enough." They hoped that I would understand and that I "wouldn't take it personally." They felt that in order for the poster to be "powerful" the central image had to be "powerful"; such a potent image, they reasoned, would require that the model "look black" and not "light-skinned" like me.

They then considered asking my husband to sit for the photo (he is darker in complexion than I am), but that idea was quickly rejected because although his "more desirable" darker image might be more potent than mine, his facial expression was "too sweet, too nice." They finally turned to an African American female acquaintance of one of the designers, whom I saw briefly prior to the photo shoot. Some days later, I saw the proofs for the poster, and the close-up photo of the woman was indeed more powerful, but she was barely recognizable from my memory of her. A dark-skinned African American woman, she was styled to look like a "black brute," reminiscent of the nineteenth-century images of African slaves being thrust onto auction blocks. In the photo, her face was greasy and beaded with perspiration. Her expression was one of extreme fatigue, misery, and distress.

Yes, the poster was powerful. Righteous indignation against the legacy of global oppression of minority peoples was indeed its tone. But as I looked at the final proof for the poster, its central image sent me reeling. Why is it that a contemporary African American must be styled to look like a brutalized slave to communicate convincingly that he or she is being oppressed? Why is only an extreme image of a black person capable of indicating that something is wrong? I wanted to scream. Must we style ourselves as brutes in order for whites to believe that we are worn down every day by discrimination?

I Q

Fifty-three percent of nonblacks believe that African-Americans are less intelligent than whites; 51 percent believe they are less patriotic; 56 percent believe that they are more violence-prone; 62 percent believe they are more likely to "prefer to live off welfare" and less likely to "prefer to be self-supporting." *

■

Another quality I like about the black world is the same thing I like about the redneck world. It's not so cerebral. It's much more hearty. In the ghetto cars frequently stop next to each other and talk. You notice it? I think, "Oh, fuck, come on, this is a street." But when I really sit back and think about it, that's a real good quality. They're saying it's not so

*   Survey on American racial attitudes, National Opinion Research Center, University of Chicago (1990).

*important to get there, but it's very important to stop and say hello. [White] people even walking on the sidewalk don't stop. And certainly not in their BMW cars.**

■

Sociologist Linda Gottfredson has used Labor Department data to com-pute the expected level of representation of blacks and whites in various fields, taking into account the level of intelligence required by the job and the differences of cognitive ability between the races. Assuming that doc-tors and engineers require IQs around 115, or that firemen and police require IQs above 85, Gottfredson calculates that when cognitive ability is taken into account, American blacks are overrepresented *in most well-paying and prestigious positions . . . Recently the* Wall Street Journal *reported that blacks hold only 2.3 percent of the almost 10,000 seats on corporate boards of large companies. Although these percentages seem low, Gottfredson argues that based on black intelligence ability as measured by IQ tests, less than 1 percent of African Ameri-cans (compared with about 20 percent of whites) qualify for success in these cognitively demanding fields.*†

■

Whenever a minority issue comes up I feel like I'm expected to say something. If I don't say something, I'm shunning my race, and if I do say something nobody listens. So you're battling with both sides of the

---

* Bill Harcliff, a thirty-one-year-old white man who works with infirmed adults, as quoted by Bob Blauner in *Black Lives, White Lives: Three Decades of Race Relations in America* (1989).
† Dinesh D'Souza, *The End of Racism* (1995).

coin. And then if you . . . say something, people think they're compli-
menting you and they say, "Wow! That's really a . . . statement!"
"That was really awesome!" "That was really intelligent!" As if I was
the first person to have ever spoken in the place. And they had no idea I
had an education. I find it very disturbing . . . *

■

Andrew Hacker, in a critique of *The Bell Curve,* asks which
white people, exactly, are genetically predisposed to score better
on IQ tests than black people. How curious, Hacker writes, that
in their analysis Herrnstein and Murray choose to treat the category of white—a catchment of more than 200 million people
in America, according to the last census—as a single, monolithic
genetic group. Extending the main argument of *The Bell*
Curve—that the variation in the IQ test scores of black and
white people can be explained genetically—Hacker wonders
how we might account for similar variations in intelligence and
intellectual accomplishments from one white ethnic group to
another. The following census figures, for example, refer to the
proportion of Americans of various European ancestries who
have completed their bachelor's degrees:

French–Canadian   16.7%
Dutch   18.5%
Italian   21.0%

---

*   A first-year black male law student at the University of Pennsylvania, as quoted by
Michelle Fine in *Off White: Readings on Race, Power and Society* (1997).

Irish   21.2%

German   22.0%

Finnish   24.2%

Norwegian   26.0%

Danish   27.4%

Swedish   27.4%

Scotch-Irish   28.2%

English   28.4%

Welsh   31.8%

Scottish   33.6%

Russian   49.0%

◼

*An evil scientist finds a way to put all white people to sleep for six decades. During this hibernation, the IQ of blacks rises three points per decade, or eighteen points. The IQ of whites stays the same. Now when the white group wakes up, it exhibits a persistent three point IQ lag behind the black group. To the social scientist, this would constitute proof that whites are "genetically" inferior to blacks. A more historical perspective would reveal that genes had nothing to do with it.**

---

* Mike Walter, "Word Problems to Take Your Mind Off the Bell Curve," in *The Bell Curve Debate: History, Documents, Opinions* (1995).

INITIATION

1

It was in college that I learned how to be a racist. It was in college that I learned that African American history and culture were irrelevant to my life. It was in college that I learned that it was in my best interest to lie about my connection to blackness. (I started telling my teachers and friends, for example, that I lived in the middle-income co-ops on Grand Street.) It was in college that I stopped studying Spanish and took up German. It was in college that I began to slick back my hair with Brylcreem. It was in college that I determined that affirmative action was bad and that blacks and Hispanics were all too often welfare cheats.

Years before I entered college, I was learning how to be a racist from my mother. Although I did not trust or respect her view of black people, I could not escape her influence altogether. I loved my mother more than anyone. I thought she was kind, and talented, and beautiful. Much like her own mother in her doting attention to my mother's career, she supported and followed my education closely. Even on her deathbed, she read every word of my honors thesis, looking for errors in grammar and spelling. Somewhere in my unconscious, I had filed away all of the facets of bigotry she had taught me. My mother's fear of blackness, a fear so visceral that it had slipped "from the conscious mind down deep into the muscles and glands" (to quote *Killers of the Dream,* Lillian Smith's brilliant autobiographical analysis of white racism in the South), was no doubt passed on to me in early childhood. I think of Smith's observation: "The mother who taught me tenderness . . . taught me the bleak rituals of keeping Negroes in their place."

Yet something in my college experience brought me closer to my mother than ever before. My first year at Hunter College was confusing. I did not immediately decry the racism around me—the racist jokes recited over lunch by fellow white students, the words "fucking nigger" used by a white student to refer to the black teenager who snatched his mother's purse, the assertion by a white teaching assistant that the writing of most black civil rights leaders was not worth reading, an offhand remark by an art history professor that "all African art looks alike"—and take up residence on the black side of the cafeteria, as I had done in high school. In college, everyone was a little older, a little more savvy, a little more adept at playing the game of racial avoidance and evasion: the black students mostly ignored me; the white students took it for granted that I was one of them.

Once, in a course on twentieth-century drama, a black student asked the unapologetically liberal white professor a not unreasonable question: Might it be interesting to compare the dashed dreams and aspirations of Willy Loman in Arthur Miller's *Death of a Salesman* (a play the professor discussed) with those of the widow Ruth Younger in Lorraine Hansberry's *A Raisin in the Sun* (a play he never even mentioned)? The teacher's reply, that Hansberry's play was "irrelevant" to his lecture, was polite enough (he was, after all, one of only two professors in the course of my college education to assign a work by a black artist: Charles Gordone's *No Place to Be Somebody*); the smirk on his face, however, revealed the contempt he felt for the student's question, if not for the student herself. Through episodes like these, I realized that my mother's views were shared by many more white people than I had imagined.

In order to break the code, to be initiated into the brotherhood of whiteness, I needed to stop fighting and start to love the wan pinkness of my skin. I flirted with the raw, unspoken power of my race, and I began to let it do its work for me.

2

My freshman adviser, a brilliant sociologist, listened patiently as I talked about the areas I wished to concentrate on in my studies at Hunter—political science, U.S. Supreme Court history, the civil rights movement, and art. She tried to convince me to change my academic concentration from the social sciences and the study of civil rights to art history and the study of modern painting and sculpture. Although she was a social scientist, my adviser felt that the world of politics, especially race politics, was too "grimy and uncreative" for my "cultivated" mind.

3

In my four years at Hunter, there was almost no discussion of the work of black intellectuals, cultural figures, or scientists in any of my classes. (Women and other people of color did not fare much better.) The conclusion to be drawn was clear: the intellectual and artistic life of black people was not something white people needed to concern themselves with. This elision recurred throughout my art historical training. I took a number of courses in college (and later in graduate school) devoted to modern abstract art. A great deal of this art, from cubism and expressionism to futurism and abstract expressionism, often appropriated—lifted, really—the style of African art. Many Western abstract painters were fascinated with the way African artists rendered the human face as an arrangement of simple geometric forms and sharp planes. The African artist depicted the face this way for various conceptual, spiritual, and ritualistic reasons. Yet when my professors lectured on the African (or South American or Oceanic) sources for modern art, they discussed them only in terms of their abstract arrangements of color and form and how these "primitive" forms and styles influenced the complex and profound compositions of Picasso and Braque. In effect, my teachers divorced tribal objects from their cultures and purposes. It was not as though such information was unavailable. By the mid-1970s, the shelves of the Hunter library held hundreds of art historical and anthropological studies of African culture.

4

In my senior year, I took a class on twentieth-century American literature taught by an eminent white poet, listened to him recite passages from the works of some of the most significant writers of the twentieth century, and never heard the words of Ralph Ellison, James Baldwin, or Richard Wright. My professor's omissions were so natural, so consistent with every other class I took in college, that I never realized that something was missing. This absence of black cultural and social figures sent a dual message: to black students, it suggested that their culture was extraneous to American culture and not worthy of study; to white students like myself, it confirmed our feelings of superiority. Such lessons made it clear that academic inquiry did not have to extend beyond the boundaries of one's own culture. From the example these lessons were setting, I was learning how to accept my whiteness, and how to preserve it.

5

From the time I first saw her on television in the early 1970s, Angela Davis captivated me. In high school, I had read her essays, admired her commanding intellect and stately bearing,

and closely followed her trial for murder, which seemed political and grossly unfair. I was ecstatic when she was acquitted. In
the mid-1970s, the student union invited Davis to speak at
Hunter. I was one of a handful of white students who attended
the lecture. As Davis spoke, in her billowing, elegant voice,
about the inequities of American politics and jurisprudence,
many of the black students cheered. I could not, did not want to
be silent. Despite the confusion and embarrassment I felt, my
heart and mind still belonged to Davis. I cheered, too. My admiration for Davis could be summed up this way: in high school
she had been a hero; in college she had become my version of
the good *schwartze*.

6

I hated the sight of her light-brown face, the part black, part
American Indian woman who beat me out of a Danforth Fellowship for graduate study. In my senior year at college, a faculty
committee was chosen to forward to the foundation a list of
four ranked nominees. I was told rather indiscreetly by one
of the committee members that I had been ranked first. The
woman of color was given the fellowship. This incident, perhaps more than any other, fueled my racism. It challenged my
sense of fairness (I was my school's top candidate, or so I
thought), and it confirmed my sense that black people required
special treatment because they were not quite as intelligent or
talented as I was. It made me envious of what I believed was
black privilege. Several of my professors and advisers (one of

whom was on the selection committee) rationalized the outcome with the following two words: "affirmative action." The Danforth evaluators, they reasoned, had settled on a less-than-superior student in order to meet a racial quota.

7

At the end of my first semester at Hunter, I walked nervously from department office to department office checking my grades, my confidence increasing with each encounter. I found myself breaking free of my father's gloomy prediction that I, like him, would never finish college. For each perfect grade, my brain also let go of a part of his iconoclasm and racial largesse. I felt as if I was choosing the possibility of success over the certainty of failure. I chose art history over political science. I chose the insider status of whiteness over the outsider status of a white boy playing at the margins of blackness. I chose to play the college game the way bright, cultivated white kids were supposed to: as an acolyte of white, male Western civilization. I chose to think and write exclusively about my own people. As my first-semester grades confirmed, I chose well.

N U R S E

In the three years between my mother's death in 1978 and my father's death in 1981, I spent a lot of time managing his illnesses. During one crisis, I rushed him to the emergency room of Beth Israel Hospital after he complained of excruciating abdominal pains. The problem was diagnosed as a massive infection. During the two weeks he spent in the hospital, I became obsessed with the interplay between my father and his "favorite nurse," as he called her. Each time she walked over to his bed, his eyes would brighten. She would tease him constantly and make jokes at his expense. He would tease and joke back. I had never seen my father show even the slightest degree of sexual attraction to a woman. Never in twenty years with my mother in a small apartment. Never in the two years since her death.

A widow in her late fifties, this nurse was about the same age my mother would have been, but the two women had little in common. My mother had been emotionally withholding; my father's nurse was affectionate and demonstrative. My mother had been overweight and weak; my father's nurse looked curvaceous and powerful in her snug white uniform. I shared his attraction to her. I was fascinated by her vivacious personality, the assured way she moved, her strong hands, her shameless sarcasm. I was attracted to her attraction to him. But I found one difference between the two women almost unbearably confusing—my mother was white and my father's favorite nurse was black.

There is no question that her blackness mattered to me. That a black woman was the object of my father's desire made it more difficult to deal with the spectacle of his lust. Her blackness, I think in retrospect, allowed me freely to change the subject of my fear from the terrifying idea of his sexuality to the more familiar, though no less difficult, issue of *her* race. My father's nurse served as the perfect scapegoat for issues that had little or nothing to do with the color of her skin. Yet her blackness, especially because it signified the racial otherness that my mother so feared and despised, enraged me.

My father's favorite nurse was the antithesis of my mother's ideal of the *schwartze* who was good because she was almost white. Her skin was dark brown; her short Afro was punctuated by strands of gray hair; her voice reverberated with traces of the South. I considered her a threat to me in much the same irrational way that white people consider black people a threat to their safety, or cultural integrity, or job security: in her presence, I was forced to think about a blackness I would have preferred to ignore. My mother's racism, combined with what I had learned from my "liberal" professors, provoked other irrational questions: How could she be smart enough for my brilliant father? What would she know about the Supreme Court, or New York politics, or the future of electric cars, or any of the things he loved to talk about? My father's fascination with her, I reasoned, could only be sexual; he needed a good fuck, I thought. And as I watched the back of her velvety brown hand gently graze and arouse the dark hairs on my father's ashen forearm, I felt disgust. I wanted to eliminate his sexuality; I wanted to eliminate her overpowering blackness.

At first, I tried to rationalize my father's passion, chalking it up to vulnerability. Patients flirt with their nurses because they are scared, trapped in their beds, hovering between consciousness and sedation, infirmity and strength. Patients come to love the conscientious (and often attractive) attendants who appear at their bedsides at signs of distress, who gently adjust their pillows, who administer their medications, who ask them how they are, who touch their bodies without asking or being asked. Despite my rationalizations, one thing confirmed the reality of the situation: I could see his naughty glint reciprocated in the eyes of his nurse.

One evening while he was still in the hospital, my father asked my sister and me if we would mind if he went out with his favorite nurse. He understood that we had recently lost our mother and that the idea of his seeing another woman or remarrying might be too much for us. Strangely, as if his own fears of intimacy had impelled him to design a convenient way out, he left the decision up to us. My sister started to cry and told him she would have trouble dealing with another woman in his life.

For me, nothing less than my mother's memory and honor, as well as the newfound purity of my own whiteness, were at stake. There could be no greater betrayal of my mother than her husband falling in love with a black woman. I played on my father's greatest fear. "Our family is fragile enough as it is," I warned. "Don't bring someone new into our lives and screw things up." I was threatening him: If you betray our mother, I will betray you. I will move out of our apartment. I will leave you with the sole responsibility of caring for your troubled daughter. I will never speak to you again.

My father, a master at manipulation himself, got the message. He never brought up his favorite nurse again.

E N V Y

On the left-hand side of the two-page advertisement in *The New York Times Magazine* is a regal head shot of a polo pony framed against a bright-blue background. His neck is long and muscular. Bound in the leather straps of the bridle, his head is a deep mahogany, with a strip of white running down the snout. His mane is closely cropped. His ears are small and rigid. His eyes glisten like black marbles. His nostrils flare. His closed mouth appears almost to be grinning.

On the right-hand side of this advertisement (for Ralph Lauren Polo shirts) is a human counterpart to the majestic horse. The man is strikingly beautiful. His head looks to the left, a perfect pendant to the right-facing horse. His skin is a deep mahogany. His elegant, shaved pate has just a hint of black stubble. His small ears curve upward and slightly away from his head. His eyes are dark and dramatic. His nostrils appear to be slightly flared; white light bounces off the bridge of his nose. His full, luscious lips seem almost to be breaking into a smile. His bright-blue shirt nearly blends into the background, giving the effect of a head and neck that graphically float, naked and powerful, against a sea of blue.

It is strange to see a black man representing a company that made its mark appealing to the American middle-class fascination with WASP wealth and taste—even if the man is Tyson Beckford, the first African American male supermodel. Beckford has been the designer's "Polo man" since March 1995, which suggests, in part, that Lauren is reaching out to prospective black customers. But juxtaposing a picture of a black man to one of an animal—the model is not wearing polo gear and is not even in the same space as the horse, suggesting that the two, rather than interacting, are being compared to each other—is an unfortunate ploy. Intentionally or otherwise, the ad replays a long-standing racist fantasy about black people: no matter how beautiful, smart, or talented, they are in some ways always exotic and animal-like.

This fantasy allows white people to feel superior to black people who they suspect may be more beautiful, more talented, or better endowed than they are. It may explain why black models are rarely seen on the cover of fashion and women's and men's magazines and why images of violent black men and irresponsible black mothers abound in the media. Positive images of black men often center on their physicality or athleticism: "Athletes, more than rappers, are more like national heroes," says Beckford's agent, Bethann Hardison. "But also, when it comes down to black men's bodies, historically it's been about how strong and well defined they are—that's what's had value. It's the same old story." The press release for a recent show of menswear by the designer John Bartlett, unusual in that it featured six black models, celebrated the special prowess of black men: "They just have a certain natural masculinity to them," Bartlett observes.

The association between blackness and innate physicality, masculinity, or naturalness often relegates black men to a less-than-human status in the media. In 1988, for example, TV sportscaster Jimmy "the Greek" Snyder offered this on-air explanation of black athletic gifts: "[T]he slave owner would breed his big black with his big black woman so that he could have a big black kid . . . The black is a better athlete to begin with because he's been bred to be that way because of his thigh size and his big size. [Blacks can] jump higher and run faster." (Snyder was later fired by CBS Sports.)

Like Lauren's vision of the black man as polo pony, such stereotypes deny the intellectual and human dimension of blackness just as surely as they systematically ascribe to black people bestial traits that are rarely applied to whites (the Marlboro Man, after all, is riding *on* his majestic horse). Sometimes this belittling of blackness is more subtle, though by no means free of the prejudices of racial biology. In 1994, for example, golfer Jack Nicklaus told an interviewer that black men have "different muscles that react in different ways" and thus were anatomically unsuited to play golf. (A few years later, of course, Tiger Woods won the U.S. Open, dispelling Nicklaus's racist assumption forever.) Nicklaus's and Synder's views of black athleticism both see athletic aptitude as inborn, physical, and even genetic; such traits as intelligence, skill, perseverance, and dedication do not come into play.

Black male models present a problem for the fashion industry, argues Hilton Als, where they "still tend to generate lurid fantasies of subway 'gangstas,' and many American designers aren't sure that black men can *sell*." Lauren has found a way out of this problem: transformed into a metaphorical satyr—half man, half horse—Beckford is freed from the specificity of contemporary black masculinity, thus making him more accessible to the white reader. This effect is also achieved, as John Hoberman points out in *Darwin's Athletes: How Sport Has Damaged Black America and Preserved the Myth of Race,* by dissolving ethnic blackness into a genteel and nonviolent "sporting world that is exclusively and impeccably white: golfing, fishing, tennis, rowing, sailing, and polo—the sports of dynamic imperial males unwinding from the rigors of colonial administration."

Yet Lauren's "Polo man" is only allowed to join this world as the counterpart to one of its beautiful, imperial animals. A handsome model, black or white, can help lure the consumer into the fantasy that buying a particular garment will grant him access to the garment's aura of beauty. The risk, however, is that the consumer may also feel competitive with or even threatened by another man's attractiveness. The very presence of black models, then, challenges the often unconscious desires of white men to see themselves as superior to black men. To some extent, Lauren neutralizes these competitive feelings by inviting us to see mirrored in the face of his mahogany "Polo man" the features of an animal prized for its physical endowments.

Too often, white people acknowledge a particular strength in a black colleague, sports figure, politician, or entertainer but dilute their recognition with the same kind of ambivalence implicit in the Lauren ad. In a study of the racial attitudes of sports reporters, for example, *Boston Globe* writer Derek Jackson analyzed the coverage of five National Collegiate Athletic Association basketball games and seven National Football League play-off games during a single season. More than three-quarters of the adjectives used to describe white football players referred to their brains, while just under two-thirds of the adjectives used for black players referred to their brawn. In basketball, the ratio was 63 percent brains for white players, 77 percent brawn for black players.

Cultural and social institutions controlled by white people have been slow to reward black accomplishment not because African Americans don't excel but because such rewards declare that a black person may, in fact, be more talented, more intelligent, or more beautiful than his white peers. One need look no further than the film industry to see white people's indifference to black people's excellence. Although African Americans buy movie tickets in disproportionate numbers (they make up 12 percent of the population but 25 percent of movie patrons), black people in Hollywood rarely achieve crossover superstar status, or are thought capable of carrying a movie, or receive such markers of success as Academy Award nominations. The 1997 Oscars were a case in point: all twenty acting nominees were white and a number of their performances were less than outstanding; overlooked were the extraordinary and critically acclaimed work of black actors Djimon Hounsou in *Amistad;* Samuel L. Jackson, Debbi Morgan, and Lynn Whitfield in *Eve's Bayou;* and Pam Grier in *Jackie Brown.* The argument, advanced by several white critics, that these films were weak and thus placed their actors at a disadvantage for Oscar nominations is specious: *Eve's Bayou* was widely praised by critics (though the film apparently did not reach white audiences) and Grier's and Hounsou's white co-stars, Robert Forster and Anthony Hopkins, were nominated. In the end, most black men in Hollywood—from Denzel Washington to James Earl Jones—remain character actors: "In other words, they are *safe*," observes actress Ellen Holly in an op-ed piece in *The New York Times* on the obstacles faced by black actors in the film industry. "They may be doing some of the most riveting work in film . . . but none is breaking the sexual taboos that keep a black man from becoming a high-wattage movie star."

Mainstream American culture's avoidance of black talent and excellence suggests one of the greatest deficiencies of whiteness: its inability to celebrate and learn from the strengths and accomplishments of black people. Too often, white people live by the rules of self-protection, competitiveness, and self-aggrandizement—rules which tell us that black men may be no more handsome or intelligent than the polo ponies on which their rich white brothers ride.

P I N K

Elizabeth Sacre, a psychoanalyst and writer, tells this story:

An Australian woman with British grandparents, an English complexion, and a few alleged drops of French Huguenot blood, I was married to a man with an African American mother, a Native American father, light-brown skin, and a flamboyantly English name. Under the circumstances, my husband contended, it would have been not only simplistic but downright untrue to call himself black and me white. If we must be defined by color, he insisted, surely he was brown and I was pink.

My husband described me once as the most unracist person he had ever known, a compliment I still find puzzling and undeserved. He attributed my lack of racism to the fact that I was Australian and hence unschooled in the ways of racial prejudice. He held to this view even after I told him about my first encounter with an Australian Aborigine in South Brisbane. A man with gray-black skin boarded the bus on which I was traveling with my mother, my sister, and my brother. I must have been seven or eight at the time, and, because we were on our way to town, I was decked out in a hat and gloves and my very best organza dress.

"Smile!" my mother ordered in a whisper as the man paid his fare, and we duly obeyed. How silly we must have looked, all four of us, grinning at a perfect stranger. He rightly ignored us as he made his way to the back of the bus. Yet I remember feeling let down. This was, I suppose, my first lesson in discrimination, however benignly intended, on the basis of skin color.

Because of when and where I grew up in Australia, such encounters were rare, so the abundance of black people (the politically correct term when I first set foot on this soil) was one of many surprises. Because I was a foreigner in the United States, my accent, my manner, and my points of reference defined me, from the start, as different. It was not until I married a "brown" man that my "pinkness" became an issue.

On most occasions, my color was embarrassingly useful. It made hailing cabs in dodgy neighborhoods a cinch, it caused waiters to be solicitous, it prevented customers in supermarkets from asking my husband or his friends, "Do you work here?" On one occasion, though, my skin color was a decided liability.

It was Christmas Eve, and I had bought a baby doll for my five-year-old niece, my husband's sister's child. The warm brown of the doll's skin matched that of my niece almost perfectly, and the color and texture of the hair were remarkably similar, too. I was shamelessly proud of my purchase, and though I dreaded parting with the doll, whom I'd grown fond of during her sojourn in my apartment, I was longing to present her to my niece.

Imagine my consternation when the little girl, having torn off the wrapping paper, flung the doll into the farthest corner of the room and shouted, "I don't want no white doll!" The doll, I realized, was white simply by virtue of its association with me.

Mother, grandmother, and uncle all tried in vain to rescue the situation, to coax, explain, make amends. But my niece stood her ground. She would have no part of the "white" doll.

I have wondered, from time to time, what happened to that doll. Was a reconciliation effected? Was she given away? Banished to the back of the closet? Conscripted to the Salvation Army? Used for target practice? All I know is I would ever so gladly have taken her home.

A F F I R M A T I V E

In 1986, when I was working on my first major project on race, an exhibition on artists who explored the issue of racism in their work, I thought a lot about the woman of color I hated so much for beating me out of a Danforth Fellowship in college. In retrospect, away from the emotions of the moment, I could be more honest about the past. My application, from the outset, was bound to fail. Not only was it sloppily typed and full of spelling mistakes, but it did not make a convincing case that I fulfilled one of the foundation's fundamental criteria—that a candidate's religious beliefs play a vital role in his or her intellectual and professional life. By my college years, I had grown to resent my rigid Orthodox Jewish upbringing and saw little connection between my religion and my work. The woman who went on to win the Danforth, also an exceptional student, had held two majors: dance therapy and religion. Early on in the

Danforth process, as we nervously chatted while waiting our turn to be interviewed by the faculty committee, she told me that she was religious and how, in her application, she had written about the connection between her spiritual life and her academic and professional life. I remember feeling envious of her: she was smart, and beautiful, and elegant, and cool. In retrospect, I doubt that the color of her skin was the reason for her Danforth success; at Hunter College, however, it cast a shadow of doubt over her intelligence, her convictions, and her talent.

FINALE

In 1954, shortly before they were married, my father informed my mother that her performing days were over. No matter that she studied voice seriously, no matter that she gave well-reviewed recitals, no matter that she continued to sing and play bit parts in the Yiddish theater: she would be the keeper of his house and the mother of his children. From that day on, my mother jealously followed the careers of others, famous opera singers. In the last year of her life, suspecting that she was dying, she allowed her bitterness to give way to a kind of sweet reverence for the discipline that had failed her so badly. She read the autobiographies of opera singers I fetched for her from the library. She listened to classical music on the radio and to the few opera records she owned. She combed *TV Guide* looking for any appearance that week by a respectable diva.

Shortly before she died, she asked me to wheel her into the living room so she could watch a concert on our color TV.

Shirley Verrett was going to appear with the New York Philharmonic on the PBS series *Live from Lincoln Center.*

Because my mother could not afford to go to the opera, television served as the link to her lost past. Verrett became one of her TV favorites through her frequent appearances in the 1960s and 1970s on the Ed Sullivan and Mike Douglas shows. To my mother, Verrett was not just a brilliant singer but an exemplary *schwartze*—so beautiful, soft-spoken, and talented, a woman who despite her rich dark brown skin was "white-acting."

My mother was excited to see the "new" Verrett sing. After years of singing mezzo parts, Verrett had recently expanded her repertoire to include soprano roles. Her *Live from Lincoln Center* performance would give my mother a chance to size up her phenomenal vocal range. This delighted my mother, herself a soprano who loved the singer more as a performer and television personality than for her mezzo repertoire. Emaciated and hunched-over in her wheelchair, my mother sat motionless as Verrett sang. Tears rolled down her face as she listened to the diva's moving finale, Mozart's "Exultate Jubilate"—a favorite recital piece from my mother's student days.

It would be the last time she got out of bed.

H A I R [3]

Renée Cox, an artist and photographer, tells this story:

White people often only see my hair; they sometimes don't even have the common courtesy or humanity to look me in the eye. I've been mistaken for every black diva at one point or another. My hair contributes to the fantasy that I am someone famous, someone safe. When I am out in the Hamptons, for instance, I am often taken for Whoopi Goldberg. I was shopping at the Amagansett Farmers Market with two friends of mine who are also African American. Two white women approached my friends and asked them if I was "her." They were so excited. "That *is* Whoopi Goldberg," they kept repeating. I don't look like Whoopi Goldberg. Our physiques are different. Our faces are different. Our skin color is different. The only thing we have in common is that we have dreadlocks.

In the summers, the East End of Long Island becomes a haven for wealthy white people. There are black people in the

Hamptons, but they keep to themselves. They don't go to the beach, the restaurants, the fancy shops; perhaps you will see a few of them at the supermarket. They're removed from the scene. Any black person that white people see in East Hampton is usually a celebrity. Why would a normal black person be coming out to the Hamptons? Everybody turns around when I walk on the main beach in East Hampton. "Oh, oh, look, that's Whoopi Goldberg, look, Whoopi Goldberg!" Always.

This doesn't only happen on Long Island. I was in a tiny bathroom in a Manhattan restaurant and I heard a woman on the phone just outside the door. She had gone into a tizzy when I walked by her a minute before. "Who is that woman who has those dead locks?" she screamed into the phone. "What do you call that thing they do with their hair, you know, when they twist it, but it's not really twisted, it's like combed together but it's long? Dreadlocks? Yeah, Whoopi Goldberg. Yeah, she just walked into the bathroom. Wow. Whoopi Goldberg is in the bathroom." And I'm sitting on the toilet thinking, "Oh my God."

Short of shaving my head, I've had my hair cut in any way a black girl can. When I wore a crew cut back in the early 1980s, people would chase me down the street screaming, "That's Grace Jones. That's Grace Jones." In the mid-1980s, I had extensions down to my ass. Extensions were still a rare thing then. White people would say "That's Chaka Khan, that's Diana Ross, that's the girl from *21 Jump Street*." Back in the 1970s, when I had Jheri curls, I was mistaken for Michael Jackson.

I could not make that kind of mistake with a white person. I wouldn't be running down the street screaming, "Oh, that's Cher," just because some white girl had long black hair; "Oh, that's Marilyn Monroe," just because she's a blonde. This behavior annoys the hell out of me. It feeds the ignorant perception that we all look alike. And it's a matter of conditioning. White people didn't have to look black people in the eye because they didn't have to deal with black people. You didn't have to look your slaves in the eye. You didn't have to look your cleaning lady in the eye. You didn't have to look the people at the back of the bus in the eye. That's why white people don't know what black people look like. And I think that's pretty heinous.

M I R R O R [2]

As I pretend to sort through my slides for the class in contemporary American art I will teach later that afternoon, I sit in the Hunter College slide library and watch, out of the corner of my eye, two professors engage in conversation. They face each other across the long wood table that takes up most of the tiny room. Their speech is polite, quiet, even respectful. She is one of my most respected colleagues. She is also a former teacher of mine. (Two years after I had graduated from Hunter, I returned as an adjunct professor in the department of art history.) He is a distinguished professor of Afro-American studies. I am fascinated and confused by their conversation: what is my former professor, a belligerently Eurocentric scholar who had never so much as mentioned the name of a black artist or intellectual, talking to this man about?

She is a short, elegant white woman in her early forties. She is wearing a camel-colored cashmere sweater, brown skirt, and an elaborately patterned dark-brown wool shawl. She is hunched slightly forward in her chair. He is a black man of about sixty and wears an elegant navy-blue suit, white shirt, and gold silk tie. His dark face is framed by short, frizzy gray hair. He wears eyeglasses and peers over the top of them. He speaks slowly and deliberately; his accent is refined, lilting, aristocratic. "The Committee on the Humanities would like to invite you to join us in planning a new humanities institute at the college," he begins. "I speak for my colleagues in saying that you are one of Hunter's most gifted professors. Your involvement would be most welcome."

"And what will this institute actually do?" she asks.

"The institute will hold regularly scheduled conferences and seminars. We will reach out to other universities. We have just as fine a faculty as Columbia University, but nobody outside of Hunter knows this. The institute will enforce the idea that we are an elite and important college."

My colleague asks for more details: "How often will the institute's board meet? Will symposia and seminars be open to the public? How will the institute be funded?"

He responds to each question patiently, offering answers that seem to satisfy my colleague: The board will meet twice a semester to set policy and programming for the institute. Symposia will be open to faculty, students, and invited guests only. ("We'll be very elite," he volunteers, invoking what seems to be one of his favorite words.) The board will be funded through general university funds as well as through solicitations from alumni, foundations, and corporations.

"It all sounds terrific," my colleague concludes, as she slowly rises from her seat, shaking her head and grinning broadly.

"Good day," he says formally as he extends his hand. "I will call you soon to follow up on our conversation."

As the man turns his back to leave, I see an immediate change in my colleague's body language. She glares at him. Her shoulders arch backward. She shakes her head. She smiles coldly. I have seen this smile before—the muscles of her face involuntarily twisting into a grin on the way to becoming a sneer. It is the contemptuous expression that erupts on her face whenever she thinks a person has said something stupid or wrong.

When he is gone, my colleague turns to me and explains what has just happened. She takes a deep breath. "How could *this* man believe that I would have *anything* to do with him or his institute?" she scoffs. "I don't get it. Who does he think he was talking to? Why would I want to have anything to do with his humanities institute?" As her voice rises, her commentary crosses the line into a mocking and scornful rant. "Humanities institute," she repeats, imitating the professor's British intonation. "Humanities institute . . . Humanities institute . . . Does he really think I would have anything to do with his humanities institute?" she says, laughing. "How frivolous. Wasn't he pretentious? What a waste of my time."

She does not wait for a response. Before I can say anything, she walks out of the slide room without saying goodbye. I am relieved because I have nothing to say to her. I have witnessed many incidents like this one, before and since. I know that the color of the man's skin matters to her; that it undermines his credibility and stature; that it renders him unworthy of her attention. I know that many white people will not pass up the opportunity to signal or share their ambivalence or incredulity about a black person to any white person in the vicinity. It is through these communications, whether they are subtle or crude, that we white people prove our loyalty to each other and to our unspoken but staunchly defended whiteness. Many white people would have handled the situation more discreetly, communicating their prejudices through an encoded repertoire of lame excuses, humorous asides, knowing glances, shrugged shoulders, rolled eyes, and nervous laughter.

In my colleague's actions and words, I see more than the bad faith of another white person. I see myself. And the mirror image of the potential of my own racist tendencies—the ugliness, the desperateness, the irrationality—stops me cold. For the first time since my college years, I am disgusted at the sight of another person's racism. Our distinguished black colleague is no less articulate, erudite, elegant, and passionate than we are. Yet the color of his skin and the subject of his scholarship mark him negatively in my professor's eyes. Strangely, they do not mark him negatively in mine.

COLOR - BLIND

The discovery of personal whiteness among the world's peoples is a very modern thing—a nineteenth- and twentieth-century matter, indeed. The ancient world would have laughed at such a distinction. The Middle Ages regarded skin color as a mild curiosity; and even up to the eighteenth century, we were hammering our national manikins into one, great, Universal Man, with fine frenzy which ignored color and race even more than birth. Today we have changed all that, and the world in a sudden, emotional conversion has discovered that it is white and by that token, wonderful!*

■

My son attends a small nursery school. Over the past year, three different teachers in his school assured me that he was color-blind. Resigned to

---

*   W.E.B. Du Bois, "On Being Black" (*The New Republic,* Feburary 18, 1920).

this diagnosis, I took my son to an ophthalmologist who tested him and pronounced his vision perfect . . .

As it turned out, my son did not misidentify color. He resisted identifying color at all. "I don't know," he would say when asked what color grass was; or, most peculiarly, "It makes no difference." This latter remark, this assertion of the greenness of grass making no difference, was such a precociously cynical retort, that I began to suspect some social complication in which he was somehow invested.

The long and the short of it is that the well-meaning teachers at his predominantly white school had valiantly and repeatedly assured their charges that color makes no difference. "It doesn't matter," they told the children, "whether you're black or white or red or green or blue." Yet upon further investigation, the very reason that the teachers had felt it necessary to impart this lesson in the first place was that it did matter, and in predictably cruel ways: some of the children had been fighting about whether black people could play "good guys."*

[I am] definitely aware of color. I think it is a superficial, comfortable response to . . . denying one's own racism, and the problem of racism in society, to say that one has become color-blind . . . The analogy that I frequently use is that, when people say, "Well, I just treat everybody the same . . ." I say that if you know that a woman has been raped, you are liable to be careful, speaking to her. You are liable to be somewhat sensitive about how you approach certain things . . . your behavior at the end of your encounter with this woman probably is such that you

---

* Patricia J. Williams, *Seeing a Color-Blind Future* (1997).

*should use it with everyone . . . It's not ridiculous behavior. You are just going to be conscious of not wanting to put salt in wounds that you recognize probably are there because of that person's experience . . . That is frequently the way I feel about interactions between blacks and whites in America. I think black people have been raped. I think they are raped, regularly, in a variety of ways.**

"What does Jessie learn when she goes up there to P.S. 2? She comes home the first day of school with a complete list of differences like a guide to a flower garden: 'In this row we've got Jews, in that row Catholics. We have a Protestant teacher and the man who cleans up after school is a Negro named Mr. Naglie and he always shouts at us to pick our papers up off the floor, so everybody calls him Mr. Nigger.'" They fought over this for a while, Jessie's father and his friends crying out for the abolition of all distinctions . . . Was it that they thought the Negro man was different from them even though they didn't believe in difference? How could that be? The whole argument, she had thought, would be something just next to lying.†

I had to meet the white man's eyes. An unfamiliar weight burdened me. In the white world the man of color encounters difficulties in the

---

* Unnamed white female respondent, in an interview with Holly Hanson, as quoted by Joe R. Feagin and Hernán Vera in *White Racism* (1995).
† Rosellen Brown, *Civil Wars* (1984).

development of his bodily schema . . . I was battered down by tom-toms, cannibalism, intellectual deficiency, racial defects . . . I took myself far off from my own presence . . . what else could it be for me but an amputation, an excision, a hemorrhage that spattered my whole body with black blood.*

---

* Frantz Fanon, *Black Skin, White Masks* (1952).

A R T I F A C T [2]

In the late 1980s I attended a panel discussion on "art and identity" at the Whitney Museum of American Art in New York City. A colleague, a white feminist scholar of nineteenth-century French art, began talking about one of that century's greatest artistic achievements—Edouard Manet's *Olympia*. The image in the foreground of the painting was both stark and radical for its time: a prostitute, pale and naked except for the hand that covers her genitals and the black ribbon tied around her neck, reclines next to her corpulent black attendant. The scholar's voice rose passionately as she indicted generations of art historians—including her own—for having ignored Victorine Meurend, the gifted artist and model who posed for Manet. Holding up a photograph of *Olympia* and pointing to the naked model, she mournfully, theatrically, and repeatedly asked, "Who was this woman? . . . Who was Victorine?" Slowly and methodically, she began to tell us who this woman was. In the course of the half-hour presentation, my colleague never once inquired about the other human being in the image, the black model named Laura, invariably left nameless and ignored by art historians.

CORNERED

The artist Adrian Piper, perhaps more than any other figure today in high or popular culture, aggressively challenges white racism. Piper's work avoids the elitist abstractions of the avant-garde in favor of gripping images and plain talk. Her installations, performances, drawings, and video pieces hold up a mirror to white viewers in radical and sometimes surprising ways.

A decade ago, Piper's video installation *Cornered,* first exhibited at the John Weber Gallery in New York City, transfixed the art world. A video monitor was situated on a stand in the corner of the room. The surrounding space was empty except for photocopies, framed and hung over the monitor, of the two birth certificates of the artist's late father—one identifying him as white, the other as black. As if to suggest a prior moment of violent dissension, an overturned table leaned against the monitor stand, its upended legs acting as a barrier between the viewer and what was to be seen on the video monitor. The artist appeared alone on-screen, shot from the torso up and sitting catty-corner in the corner of a room that was uncannily synchronized with the space around the video monitor in the gallery. Piper's hair was pulled back in a chignon; she wore a conservative blue dress, delicate earrings, and a strand of pearls. Her tone was impersonal, neutralized, much like that of an anchorwoman on a television news program or like a no-nonsense voice-over in a public service announcement.

Piper's precious junior-miss style and unemotional delivery belied her very provocative words. A light-skinned black woman who (like her father) could easily pass for white, Piper announced at the outset: "I'm black." For the next twenty minutes, the viewer was increasingly, almost claustrophobically, cornered by her words. Explaining why passing for white would be an act of self-hatred and self-degradation, Piper reminded viewers that "the problem is not just my personal one, about my racial identity. It's also your problem, *if* you have a tendency to behave in a derogatory or insensitive manner toward blacks when you see none present."

Within moments, she really got to the heart of the matter. If, as some researchers estimate, almost all purportedly white Americans have between 5 and 20 percent black ancestry, then why shouldn't most Americans be classified as black? "What are you going to do about it," she asked. "Are you going to tell your friends, your colleagues, your employer that you are, in fact, black, not white, as everyone had supposed?" Piper's questions pulled the white viewer into a web of confrontation and self-analysis. At the opening reception for the piece, one man loudly protested, "Nobody's going to tell me I'm not white."

Piper is keenly aware that it is much easier to look at art than to face the realities of one's own bigotry. Nevertheless, over the past thirty years, her work has uncomfortably reflected on the human impulse to use stereotypes to rationalize primitive fears and suspicions. Perhaps no contemporary artwork is more successful in dealing with racism in everyday life than Piper's *My Calling (Card) #1 (For Dinners and Cocktail Parties)* (1986–1990). The work consists of a small printed card, designed for distribution at dinner and cocktail parties. Whenever a white guest would make, laugh at, or agree with a racist remark, she would hand him or her one of the cards, which read:

Dear friend,

I am black.

I am sure that you did not realize this when you made/laughed at/agreed with that racist remark. In the past, I have attempted to alert people to my racial identity in advance. Unfortunately, this invariably causes them to react to me as pushy, manipulative, or socially inappropriate. Therefore my policy is to assume that white people do not make these remarks, even when they believe that there are no black people present, and to distribute this card when they do.

I regret any discomfort my presence is causing you, just as I am sure you regret the discomfort your racism is causing me.

Sincerely yours,

Adrian Margaret Smith Piper

Piper's calling card discreetly encourages people to think about the potential of their racist words to hurt, to alienate, to violate. When Piper publicly discusses her motives for handing out the card—as she does in special meta-performances in which she talks about the card and its repercussions with specially assembled discussion groups across the country—white middle- and upper-middle-class members of the audiences most often respond defensively. This problem, of course, is almost impossible to avoid when the subject of race enters a discussion. A videotape of a meta-performance at the Randolph Street Gallery in Chicago in 1987, in which a mostly white audience interacts with Piper, is particularly revealing. As Piper lectures on the race calling card, the audience becomes visibly agitated: nervous laughter can be heard as people shift uncomfortably in their seats. White members of the audience seem particularly worried about how it might feel to receive one of these cards. Piper's strategies are scrutinized, and she is admonished for humiliation-causing behavior and barraged with defensive questions and comments:

> Is the point of your card to tell [white people] that
>   they're no good?
> It's hard to get around this kind of policing action.
> Handing a person a card is condescending.
> None of us want to be reduced to our most [de]based
>   acts.
> To what extent is your *card* racist?
> I see racism in the uniformity of your card. Each act
>   should be dealt with individually.
> Don't you think you should inject some humor into
>   your cards?

Are you thinking about a better way to encourage
 response?
You are in a very unique situation. You are very light-
 skinned, so you could pass for a white person.
Aren't you really looking for [white] people to give
 these cards to?

It is not until much later that members of the audience
address the positive side of the consciousness-raising exercise. It
is not until the final, and most effective, minutes of the performance that a white woman asks Piper what it feels like to hand
someone one of her cards: "It ruins my evening," she answers. It
is only then that the negative questions and comments stop, that
the audience drops its guard and a kind of sadness enters the
room.

... It may be more difficult for white people to say "Whiteness has nothing to do with me—I'm not white" than to say "Race has nothing to do with me—I'm not a racist" ... To speak of whiteness is ... to assign *everyone* a place in the relations of racism.

—Ruth Frankenberg, *White Women, Race Matters: The Social Construction of Whiteness*

Whiteness is rarely discussed in American life and culture. White people, while vigilantly aware of the presence of blackness, are most often oblivious to the psychological and political weight of their own color. Black people cannot help but evaluate the status of their blackness in relation to the racism they experience every day. White people usually take the entitlements of their skin color for granted.

For many white Americans, racism is the black person's fantasy; it is a past sin that is no longer a serious problem. Half a century ago, many white people wore their racism as a badge of honor; today, few whites are willing to admit to *any* racist feelings at all. As the historian Manning Marable observes, contemporary racism is "most keenly felt in its smallest manifestation." Middle-class African Americans now endure a racism that is generally far less virulent than in earlier times but no less real:

white merchants who drop change on the counter rather than touch their hands; cabdrivers who bypass them to pick up white passengers across the street; white salespeople who, assuming they have no money, patronize them in jewelry stores and automobile showrooms; and security guards who follow them around department stores and malls.

The message of these gestures, though it may be encoded, is clear and infuriating to black people, telling them that they are considered inferior to whites. This message is further reinforced by the relentless indifference and prejudice of American social, cultural, and political institutions: by an overwhelmingly white Congress bent on dismantling three decades of social welfare programs; by police officers who routinely harass black motorists; by banks that redline entire neighborhoods; by advertising agencies that forget that African Americans spend money too; by workers in national restaurant chains who refuse to serve black patrons; by television networks that continue to segregate the races through "black" and "white" programming; by mainstream museums that schedule token exhibitions for Black History Month and ignore the art of African Americans for the rest of the year; by a publishing industry that employs few black editors; by educational systems that embrace self-fulfilling prophecies of black failure or stupidity; by a medical establishment that is insufficiently concerned with black patients' comparatively poor survival rates for cancer, heart disease, and strokes. These clear, unambiguous instances of white people's indifference and hostility continually remind African Americans that the scourge of racism has not been eliminated nor is it under control. Such misdeeds reflect a structure of "power, privilege, and violence which most blacks can never forget," to quote Marable, and which most whites cannot even see.

White people have much to gain (but ultimately much to lose) by not acknowledging the benefits of their skin color. Whiteness is not just a genetic, biological, or cultural category; it is one of society's most imperious signifiers of power and status. Whiteness has been so coveted and protected that well into this century legal standards existed to ferret out blackness even in the whitest of our brothers and sisters. Only those who could prove a kind of racial purity—a purity that as little as one drop of African blood would sully—had a legitimate claim to their whiteness. While the social implications of whiteness remain mostly unspoken today, race is no less meaningful to white people who continually reinforce their own authority and social standing by seeing themselves in positive contrast to an inferior, negative, or even dangerous blackness. Whiteness, on the other hand, is pure and value-free. It is innate; it is everywhere.

It is important to acknowledge that whiteness is not a univalent category. The strengths and limitations of one's own whiteness depend on many factors; its power and privileges are not awarded evenly or evenhandedly. Like blackness, whiteness is at best an imprecise term. Like blackness, whiteness is culturally, socially, politically, and economically diverse. Like blackness, whiteness connotes multiple meanings, multiple ethnicities, multiple shades of pink, and brown, and yellow. Like blackness, whiteness can be divided into dissonant or even warring factions. And blackness and whiteness, through centuries of miscegenation, can blend together into racially ambiguous hues that defy our society's racial categories.

Other factors can bring into question the power of white-ness. Forms of prejudice other than racism—anti-Semitism, sexism, scorn of homosexuals, class bias—can be turned against white people, threatening their authority and fostering deep feelings of powerlessness. Most white people, poor and middle-class, also suffer the anxieties of ungratifying jobs or shaky finances. It is getting even harder to convince them that white-ness matters, that it is profitable, that it gives them power.

That middle- and working-class white people are no less oppressed by the interests of big business or government than African Americans, however, does not detract from the fact that even poor whites have historically been able to capitalize on their whiteness. Nineteenth-century European immigrants who initially defined themselves as Irish, German, or Italian eventually came to embrace the idea that they were white Americans. The white ruling class, responding to agrarian and labor unrest among eighteenth- and nineteenth-century immigrants, increasingly advocated the notion of racial solidarity. Manipulating workers into accepting the myth of an endangered white race, employers granted racial privileges to propertyless white workers to encourage their alliance with the white bourgeoisie and to pacify any opposition to black slavery. W.E.B. Du Bois argued in his groundbreaking *Black Reconstruction in America* that white workers knowingly exchanged unnecessarily low wages for a "sort of public and psychological wage. They were given deference because they were white. They were admitted freely with all classes of white people to public functions, public parks, and the best schools"—privileges that did little in the short term to improve their economic standing.

A century later, whiteness continues to afford white Americans (the rich, the middle class, and even, to an extent, the poor) an almost constant dividend—the ability to live their lives without having to think about the color of their skin. While other factors might endanger us, our race does not generally threaten our survival or well-being; nor does it provide us with a daily barrage of suspicious glances, physical and emotional evasion, closed doors, and thoughtless comments and insults. Although white people may also be hobbled by prejudice, poverty, or alienation, we can usually count on our whiteness to grant us freer access to a social sphere that is controlled by white people. Merchants will place change directly in the palms of our hands. Teachers will not take our stupidity or ignorance for granted. Cabbies will stop for us. Salespeople will not automatically assume that we are poor or thieves. Banks will not keep us out of segregated neighborhoods. Terrorists will not firebomb our churches. And security guards will not see in each of us the face of a criminal.

T H E M

Leland Wheeler, a social worker, tells this story:

When Columbia University informed me that my first social-work field placement was in Harlem, I panicked. I feared violence, even death. The only other white person working in the agency—a center specializing in helping formerly homeless women integrate into the community—was, like myself, a social worker in training. Meeting my clients for the first time, I didn't know how to be. I was nervous. I was supposed to be helping these people and I felt like I was flying by the seat of my pants. I thought that they were suspicious of a white male trying to help them. How would they deal with a white person when (and this was my projection) they saw white people as the enemy?

One thing I did helped to win their trust: I started a reading group where we read and discussed writing by black women about problems and triumphs in their lives. We read a number of authors—including Maya Angelou, J. California Cooper, Rita Dove, Nikki Giovanni, and Jamaica Kincaid—many of whom I had never read before. I also started using my sense of humor. When I joked with these women, I was being real. We could connect there. I appeared more human. It was through my humor that I was able to convey to them how much I did understand. The fact that I was comfortable enough to joke about their problems meant that I knew where they were coming from.

I was also upset by my initial interaction with my black colleagues. Although I liked my supervisor, I never felt comfortable with the fact that she was very religious. I thought that her constant talking about "the good Lord" was really inappropriate. One of the other things I had problems with was all the staff parties. It seemed like we were having a party every week. They would bring in the fried chicken and Chinese food, and we'd have lunch together, and there would be a group prayer. And I kept thinking, this isn't right.

Most of my black colleagues were friendly but kind of distant. The men were particularly difficult and suspicious. The motivation I showed toward my clients, however, eventually helped me to win my colleagues' trust. They perceived how much I was enjoying my interactions with these women, that I wasn't just enduring the white man's burden. Over time, my colleagues became more forthcoming, more trusting, more helpful. I'd hear more about their families and their private lives. They'd talk about difficulties with work and the problems of making ends meet.

My discomfort didn't die easily. I had never before been so aware of the color of my skin. I was swimming in a sea of difference, and I really knew it. I was white. WHITE. Simply knowing this, however, did not lessen my sense of superiority. I was very opinionated in case conferences and discussions. I was in that white-male "I'm going to fix this, I have the answer" mode. During one of the discussions, I had an idea. But I didn't say it. About a minute later, someone else said it. I suddenly realized that I was not the smartest thing on earth. Other people were just as smart. And just because I was white and male did not mean that I was the most capable person in the room.

In the end, I think I imagined a lot of things. I imagined that they didn't like me or were afraid of me. Their blackness made me nervous. I was surprised at my response; I thought I had worked through a lot of my fears and biases toward black people. But I couldn't find a comfortable place for myself. I finally realized that I was a new person in their space and I was the one who needed to calm down. I think that they picked up on my fear and ambivalence and that fueled their fears and discomfort. In retrospect, as far as entering a new place and finding my niche and fitting in, my experience was rather standard. Once I felt comfortable with myself, things worked out really well. In the end, my field placement was a wonderful and revealing experience. The staff even threw me a birthday party—one of those lunches that I had thought were wrong and had not understood. Now, one of these parties had become mine, and it felt wonderful.

KNOWING

Many whites seem to have a strong feeling that African Americans are somehow not like white people . . . One white professional summarized the point of view: "I think it's just a matter of values, of blacks having lower standards and lower values than whites, if you're going to put it black versus white." One striking thing about negative white commentaries is that very rarely is the law-abiding majority of black America mentioned, much less given credit for surviving under serious economic and racial difficulties. Reality is sacrificed for sincere fictions; most whites' lack of empathy makes them unable to relate to the black struggle to survive in a hostile world.*

■

* Joe R. Feagin and Hernán Vera, *White Racism* (1995).

I went to a dinner party where a young white woman who seemed to be an admirer of my work wanted to sit next to me . . . but immediately she said, "I'm having problems with my black woman roommate, and I just wanted to know if you could tell me why she's behaving this way." I replied, "You know, if you wanted to know about Buddhism, would you grab the first Buddhist priest you met and say, 'Really, tell me all about it in the space of a half hour'?" I think that often when it comes to race or meaning across *difference, people just lose their rational capacity to know how to approach something—I think a lot of white people give up their power of knowing.**

Without significant exception the universalizing discourses of modern Europe and the United States assume the silence, willing or otherwise, of the non-European world. There is incorporation; there is inclusion; there is a direct rule; there is coercion. But there is only infrequently an acknowledgment that the colonized people should be heard from, their ideas known.†

*   bell hooks, *Outlaw Culture: Resisting Representations* (1994).
†   Edward Said, *Culture and Imperialism* (1993).

D I A L O G U E

On December 3, 1997, as part of his "national conversation on race," President Clinton convened a "town hall" meeting in Akron, Ohio. As the event proceeded, audience members touched on the question of race in ways that were either platitudinous (the need to encourage tolerance) or just plain vague. Fearing that the discussion was disintegrating into banal chatter, Clinton asked participants to be "blunt and brief." Since neither honesty nor brevity was forthcoming, the President made a dramatic and provocative gesture. He walked up to Abigail Thernstrom—one of America's most vehement opponents of race- and gender-based preferences who was invited to the meeting after Clinton's race initiative was criticized for excluding conservatives—and asked her a question: "Abigail, do you favor the United States Army abolishing the affirmative action program that produced Colin Powell? Yes or no?"

As the audience tittered uncomfortably, Thernstrom struggled with an answer. She began by questioning whether General Powell needed special preferences to succeed. The President, clearly unsatisfied with Thernstrom's attempt to divert the question, asked again whether she would favor abolishing the Army's affirmative action program.

"Yes or no?" he prodded.

Clearly thrown by Clinton's question, Thernstrom could give only a muddled reply. "We should . . . the Army does one thing very, very right," she began. "It prepares kids, it takes kids before the Army and it prepares them to compete equally." She went on to say that racial "preferences disguise the problem"—the "racial skills gap," as she called it—that makes some people truly unequal.

Thernstrom's answer, confused as it was, was exactly what Clinton wanted. The President's ploy—to reveal the complexity of the question of affirmative action by exposing the weaknesses of its opponents' knee-jerk arguments—was a media success. The next day, newspapers and TV news programs across the country proclaimed that Clinton had scored a knockout.

The incident was one of the few exemplary moments in the recent history of American discourse on race. It revealed a great deal about the power of strong, resolved leadership—in this case, the guidance of a sitting President who has obviously thought a lot about race—to help undo our stubborn assumptions about race. Clinton's actual reply to Thernstrom's muddled comments—he argued that the Army's egalitarian training did not adequately prepare soldiers for the unequal treatment they might receive in the civilian world—was far less significant or convincing than his rattling the opposition on one of its most hallowed issues. Clinton had thrown Thernstrom off balance simply by asking one of America's most entrenched and polemical racial questions.

Most public initiatives on race—including the President's own, which has been largely unfocused and ineffective—are doomed to fail because they cannot get beyond most people's stock responses, blind spots, and limitations. When the President's National Advisory Board on Race, headed by the esteemed historian John Hope Franklin, excluded opponents of affirmative action from its earlier debate, for example, it unwittingly undermined one of its greatest challenges: to work beyond the intractable, narrow views of race held by most Americans. Most people, white or black, will not be persuaded to change their minds simply because a quasi-official committee bombards them with a point of view that they have already rejected.

While I am not optimistic about the potential of these conversations to change people's minds, I think it is possible for some Americans to change the way they think about race. For one, we must be honest about the extreme limitations of these conversations. Too often, the people in charge, even President Clinton himself, idealize them as the means by which Americans of all colors will work out their differences once and for all. The subject of race does not lend itself to easy answers, or even to answers at all. As the Akron town meeting underscored, one person's understanding of affirmative action as a remedy for centuries of bigotry and oppression could be turned around and just as adamantly, stubbornly, irreversibly serve as another's example of reverse discrimination.

Discussions of race in America, dependent as they are on clichés and conventional wisdom, are rarely as finessed or complex as they need to be. Most of these—whether in the form of town meetings, TV panel discussions, or consciousness-raising groups—are set up as a reaction to a big, sensational incident, such as the trial of O. J. Simpson or the beating of Rodney King by the Los Angeles police. Their relevance remains intact only until the fire burns down and the incident recedes into the past; their effect tends to be fleeting and, more often than not, predictably divisive.

Much of the debate around the Simpson case, for example, centered on self-fulfilling prophecy of a nation polarized by race. In a televised town meeting on the Simpson criminal verdict, for example, *Nightline* opened with video footage that clearly illustrated this divergence: on one side of the screen, a group of black people, watching a live broadcast of the verdict, cheered as Simpson was declared not guilty; on the other side, white people, viewing the same broadcast in a different community, cried out in disbelief. These images set the tone of the rest of the show: few commentators could get beyond the idea of a nation divided.

Not everyone's attitude about the case was as fixed. Many Americans, white and black, believed Simpson was guilty and blamed the failure to convict him not on a racist black jury but on an inept prosecution, sloppy handling of evidence, and the questionable practices of overzealous policemen. Many African Americans, some of them the victims of police misconduct, found it difficult to believe the testimony of law-enforcement officers yet were never really sure of Simpson's guilt or innocence.

Indeed, as numerous public-opinion polls reported, not all black people believed Simpson was innocent; and not all white people believed he was guilty, including the criminal trial's two white jurors.

Most discussions of race in America inadequately consider the vulnerability and fragility of their participants. Choosing to talk about race in public is a difficult, even brave, act. Most of us are reluctant to talk about race in the first person, let alone in dialogue. In 1994, I was the host of a popular on-line conference on race. Participants argued. They vented. They even bolted at times. Yet our talk repeatedly turned to the kind of hot-button race issues usually avoided in polite conversation: money, quotas, resentment, guilt, the failure of integration, black separatism, white belligerence, black rage, personal incidents of racial tension, and white moral responsibility for centuries of slavery and discrimination. Sometimes we drifted into personal squabbles; other times we were provoked or even moved. Sometimes the conference seemed astonishingly honest and successful, appealing to our empathy and bringing us closer to our own anxieties about race and racism. Other times it appeared to be no more than a bunch of white people indulging in abstract thinking.

After a while, however, I began to suspect that the conversation was not entirely new for many of the participants—activist graduate students, artists, and writers. Most of them, I'm now convinced, would never have chosen to join the conference if they had not already done some private and constructive soul-searching about race. This insight suggests a significant and daunting problem with the idea of a national conversation on race: most Americans are simply not ready to talk about these things in public. Even before we can talk to each other, we must first think for ourselves about things that embarrass or upset us—in private, where we can be honest and not fear humiliation or retribution.

Ultimately, the politics of the individual is central to the politics of race. Virtually all aspects of life and culture can play a role in the formation of racial attitudes: the ancestors who make up our ethnic past; the parents, relatives, and siblings we grow up with; the teachers and clergy who guide and instruct us; the colleagues we work with; the friends and neighbors we live with; the television, videos, and films we watch; the music we listen to; the books, magazines, and newspapers we read. Thus, the process of self-inquiry into our own behavior, the act of delving deeply into the meaning of these personal and public influences and our own actions, is crucial to understanding how racism is constructed and how it operates.

Over the past decade, I have talked to hundreds of people about race. Most of these discussions were casual, conducted without a tape recorder. Few of these encounters, particularly those with white people, were all that honest or revealing. Most of the black people I talked to, although reluctant to discuss the painful racism they had experienced, were at least willing to talk about their own racial attitudes—even to the extent of sharing their past and present feelings of hostility toward white people. White people, on the other hand, usually refused to admit their own complicity in the racist incidents they recalled.

Indeed, most people will do almost anything to preserve the comfortable illusion of themselves as free of prejudice. An infamous 1990 CBS News/*New York Times* poll demonstrated this tendency: while only 19 percent of New York City residents said they used racial slurs, 50 percent said they knew others who did. White people appear to be especially sensitive to the charge of racism. In an effect that pollsters describe as "racial skewing," for example, many white voters mislead pollsters in surveys of elections in which a white candidate is running against a black one. In such elections, the black candidate usually wins far fewer votes than those forecast by most surveys, even exit polls conducted on election day. Political analysts suggest one principal reason for this discrepancy: some white voters, wishing to avoid looking racist, claim to support a black candidate and then do not vote for him or her.

In attempting to undo our bigotry, it is ultimately these personal, and somewhat banal, attitudes that are our greatest enemy. To be honest about race demands that one be honest about one's racial attitudes. The fear of revealing these dirty secrets has hindered race talk for decades. The irony is that it is only by revealing such secrets that race talk can be effective. It might make better sense for those officials, teachers, and institutions committed to improving race relations in America to encourage self-inquiry on the most personal, rather than the most public, level. Teachers should encourage students, even young children, to think about race in personal and specific terms, helping them to explore their own attitudes about racial differences as well as those of their parents, classmates, and the media. Political leaders should make the kinds of bold, direct gestures made by President Clinton in Akron—acts that stimulate individual thinking about race because they speak so uncompromisingly to the core issues that inform almost every-one's opinions on race. Television producers and writers, capi-talizing on the already intimate relationship between viewer and television screen, should introduce more honest depictions of racial interaction and personal racism in their dramas, situation comedies, talk shows, and children's programming. The unique character of on-line communication can make it an important forum for people—especially white people, given the relative whiteness of cyberspace—to talk about race more or less anonymously and free of the kinds of anxieties that face-to-face discussions provoke. Instead of advocating national conversa-tions, town meetings, and other *public* discussions on race, the President should encourage Americans to be blunt with them-selves. Nothing less will prepare us for the difficult conversations on race, both public and private, that undoubtedly lie ahead.

T R E A S O N

Michele Wallace, a cultural critic and professor, wrote me:

Dear Maurice,

. . . When it comes to race, even the best people aren't particularly good. This is precisely why so little progress is made,
despite all the discussion on race. Most people are not coming
from an informed or enlightened place. They are coming from
ignorance and bad faith. Not necessarily their own bad faith, but
bad faith they have inherited from those who came before
them: old friends, family, the books they read, the movies they
see. As for you, my friend, I think that you should be aware that
when a white person decides to closely align himself with
antiracist positions, arguments, and colleagues, there is a degree
to which the pariah status of the abject other (in this case, the
racial other) rubs off. This is particularly the case with you
because you are juggling multiple categories of abjection (an

identification with poverty based on your family history, Jewishness, gayness, progressive politics, empathy for women, and so forth). Race is, in fact, culturally and socially constructed; it is entirely possible to do things, say things, and write things that will land you as firmly in the "not white" camp as if you had been born there. I think this is why white folk are incessantly engaged in doing and saying things to identify themselves as a part of the dominant racism. I believe they need to do this in order to trust one another. There is a lot of suspicion for any white person who consistently doesn't do this, oddly enough, particularly in a high-powered, cosmopolitan, competitive environment like New York. You are going to catch all kinds of hell when your book comes out. White folk will say things to you they wouldn't dream of saying to a black author, so you mustn't be sensitive or squeamish. You must let them see your strong, tough side because that is the only thing they are ever going to respect. Don't try to appeal to their empathy, because most of them haven't got any . . .

Love,
Michele

D E N I A L

Jews are the most racist of all white people," a friend's husband announces during a conversation we are having about race. I am stunned. Of the white people with whom I've discussed this subject over the past several years, he is one of the most receptive. He tells me at the outset that he believes white racism is still a serious problem. "Racists are ugly," he volunteers. "They're ruining any chance that black people will come to trust white people."

"Jews are the worst," he claims. "By far. At work, they're the first ones to use racist slurs and to be unfairly critical of blacks. Jews are the first to talk behind their black colleagues' backs."

"You shouldn't make generalizations like that," I shoot back. "Jews were at the forefront of the civil rights movement. Some of them were killed defending the rights of black people. Many Jews still support things like affirmative action and racial justice.

Yes, there are plenty of Jews who don't like blacks, but no more or less than any other white people."

Although he nods his head in agreement, I sense that I am still not getting through. He has witnessed what he has witnessed, and my observations are not going to convince him otherwise. Privately, I wonder why he has chosen to single out Jewish racism in my presence. Is he insensitive to my Jewishness? Is all this discussion about race making him uncomfortable? Is he trying to shut me up or turn the question of racism away from himself? Is he, the altruistic, liberal WASP, putting me in my place? Is he being competitive? Or is he making what he believes to be a reasonable, and perhaps useful, observation— that a lot of Jews he encounters are unusually racist?

His observation raises an even more important question: How different are his attitudes about race from those of his Jewish colleagues and friends? I do not ask this question abstractly; I do not intend it as a comparative exercise in the personal or ethnic politics of race. Rather, I ask the question because I sense that his reference to Jews was in part defensive, in part projection. A year earlier, I had attended his wedding. What was most disturbing to me about that event—a lush and glamorous affair, with white linens and pale roses, held at an old-line WASP country club that was, until very recently, restricted—was its relentless whiteness. Of the two hundred invited guests, not one was black. The entire service staff was white, save for a black member of the band who doubled as a waiter. I had entered a realm of WASP proscription and intolerance that made me, a Jew who might well have been the target of this intolerance, as uncomfortable as it made my hosts feel right at home.

That discomfort returns to me as I listen to this soft-spoken and intelligent man condemn his gauche and insensitive Jewish colleagues. It is not the veracity of his words that I question, but his understanding of what constitutes the most egregious forms of racial prejudice. Racism that is passive and unspoken is apparently easier to ignore; only in its emotive and articulated form is racism worthy of notice and condemnation. In effect, he can protest loudly only the racism he can see or, more probably, wants to see. Jewish racism against blacks does indeed exist, but I think he protests too much. His own racism—the racism of his parents, the racism of his ancestors, the racism of his teachers, the racism of his friends, the racism on which WASP power and capital have been built and perpetuated—he does not, cannot protest at all.

FEAR

I've been wonderin' why
Peoples livin' in fear
Of my shade
(Or my hi top fade)
I'm not the one that's runnin'
But they got me on the run
Treat me like I have a gun
All I got is genes and chromosomes
Consider me black to the bone
All I want is peace and love
On this planet
(Ain't that how God planned it)*

■

* Public Enemy, "Fear of a Black Planet" (1990).

It's a horrible, sadistic thing that Washington tells whites, "You have to send your kids to school with blacks so they can beat them up." Don't white kids have any rights? It's terrible to make them go to school with blacks, who are intellectually inferior and misbehave in class. You know, my son is transferring to [a very selective public high school] this fall. They've got a special program for blacks. I just hope they leave him alone . . . I've been mugged many times. The whole bit: knives, guns. Blacks just have fewer inhibitions, a greater readiness to express anger, an impulsiveness. It fuels this incredible idea that you see something you want and shoot somebody to get it. What do they do that for? Because the alternative—to work and save—is not psychologically available. [*]

Willie Horton has taught me the continuing need for a skill W.E.B. Du Bois outlined and perfected 100 years ago: living with the veil. I am recognizing my veil of double consciousness, my American self and my black self. I must battle, like all humans, to see myself. I must also battle, because I am black, to see myself as others see me; increasingly, my life, literally, depends upon it. I might meet Bernhard Goetz on the subway; my car might break down in Howard Beach; the armed security guard might mistake me for a burglar in the lobby of my building. And they won't see a mild-mannered English major trying to get home. They will see Willie Horton. [†]

[*] Philosophy professor Michael Levin of the City College of New York, as quoted by Adam Miller in "Professors of Hate," in *The Bell Curve Reader* (1995).
[†] Anthony Walton, "Willie Horton and Me" (*The New York Times Magazine,* August 20, 1989).

BISCUITS

Therese Lichtenstein, a writer and college professor, tells these stories:

It was the early 1950s. I was about four years old. My aunt and uncle had a chicken farm in New Jersey, and my family and I would visit them twice a year. They had a big old farmhouse filled with quilts, featherbeds, and apple pies cooling on a windowsill. I loved being there, walking in fields of wildflowers, feeding the animals, and playing with my cousins. Black day workers often worked on the farm. Many times when we were driving there, we would see these black families, grownups and children, walking along the road. My father frequently gave them a lift; it was a long and tedious walk from the station. I often played with black children on the farm and became very friendly with one little girl who was about the same age as I was. I would play with her whenever we visited the farm.

One summer day, in the late afternoon, my aunt called me to the back stairs outside the kitchen to give me a dish of strawberry ice cream. I eagerly ran over to her with my friend and started to share the ice cream with her. As soon as my aunt saw me do this, she screamed: "That ice cream isn't for her. These children aren't supposed to eat ice cream. They eat dog biscuits. They can only have dog biscuits." I felt very protective toward this little girl and ashamed and humiliated for her. We ran back to the dusky workers' shack and I gave her the ice cream. I asked her if she really ate dog biscuits for snacks. She told me that she did. She took one from the cupboard. I wanted to try one and bit into the rock-hard, tasteless biscuit, wondering how a dog could eat it. Even as a four-year-old, I knew it was the color of the little girl's skin that compelled my white aunt to treat her like an animal. And I felt anger and disgust toward my aunt.

A few years ago, I was riding home on the Long Island Rail Road. As I boarded the Manhattan-bound train, I noticed that the car contained only one other passenger: a black male in his thirties or early forties. He was sitting in the rear of the car. I was sitting near the front of the car. I felt uncomfortable. While I'm usually anxious when I'm the only other person in an empty car, I felt especially so because the man was black. I will admit that if he had been dressed in a suit, instead of like a homeboy, I would have been less afraid. I felt that he, too, could look at me and easily project negative things about my color or my racism. But still I conjured up in my mind the negative stereotype of the dangerous black man. I felt very vulnerable as a white woman. I felt that he could do anything to me. I thought he might hold me up with a knife or a gun. I thought that he was going to rob me, or murder me, and that he would get away with it because there would be no witnesses. I didn't want him to think I was afraid of him; I thought that if I showed any sign of fear he would attack me.

I really started to get scared when he moved from the back of the car to the middle. He was inching toward me, moving further up. I was petrified. I did what I usually did in situations when I'm frightened—I started talking to break the charged silence. I tried to be as matter-of-fact and upbeat as possible, so he wouldn't pick up on my fear. I said, "Hi." He said hello back. We started talking. He ended up sitting across from me and we continued talking. It was like we were strangers sitting across from each other in a waiting room or on a plane, biding our time with conversation.

Before long, he didn't seem dangerous. I actually began to like him. I thought he was a nice and sensitive guy. I felt guilty: I wanted him to know that I wasn't afraid of him and that I wasn't afraid of black men. I started talking about racism with him. I told him I was a college professor and that I often discussed African American culture and race in my classes. He seemed completely interested. We formed a bond. I can't remember what he did for a living. But I think we were both astonished at how the wall of suspicion and fear that had separated us had fallen. He seemed relieved that I had talked to him and that I wasn't targeting him as some kind of murderer or thief.

I don't know why he started inching up toward me in the first place. Maybe he really did want to intimidate me. Or maybe he was uncomfortable with my fear and wanted to alleviate his anxiety. The experience turned out to be a kind of epiphany for both of us. As I think about it now, I'm not sure that I still wouldn't be just as scared if I were to experience a similar incident tomorrow.

H O T E L S

I am standing in the lobby of a once-grand hotel in Baltimore that is now a bit shabby. An autographed picture of Vice President Quayle (the year is 1989) hangs over the concierge's desk. I am serving as a one-man welcoming committee, greeting fellow panelists at a symposium I have organized on the history of performance art. I call to old friends and colleagues and search for the participants I have never met as they make their way through the large brass-and-glass revolving doors. I am the consummate academic, congratulating each person on his or her most recent book, dance piece, or film.

I notice a tall, lean black man walking through the lobby. He looks confused and a little out of breath. His dreads are dramatic. He is wearing a dark-blue jacket, a wrinkled white shirt, opened at the neck to reveal an African medallion, and jeans. He cranes his long neck, obviously searching for someone or something. He looks nervous. He sits down on the tired sofa a few feet in front of where I'm standing. I continue greeting my guests.

I notice that he is beginning to look at me. When he gets up from the sofa and approaches me, I grow apprehensive. Who *is* this man? He looks lost. He looks nervous. He is sweating. Who *is* this man? He begins to open his mouth. Who *is* this man? I'm still apprehensive. Who *is* this man? As he opens his mouth to ask me a question, I instinctively begin to shake my head no. I catch myself, but maybe not soon enough. "You must be Professor Berger," he stammers, and introduces himself as one of my panelists.

I am checking into one of Washington's most expensive hotels. I am in town to give a lecture on racism in American culture at the Washington Project for the Arts (WPA), one of the city's most important alternative spaces. The hotel has donated a suite to the WPA—a gesture of goodwill toward the contemporary-arts community and presumably, because my lecture will deal principally with race, toward the city's African Americans. I grow uncomfortable as the concierge, finishing his gracious but obsequious welcome, stares at me oddly. "The WPA asked me to give you this," he says, his eyes still scrutinizing my face as he hands me a press release about my lecture. Several minutes later, relaxing in my room, I read the press release. Its first sentence explains the concierge's quizzical expression: "Maurice Berger, an African American art historian from Hunter College in New York, will discuss the issue of race and culture in American life in a special lecture at the WPA."

■

I arrive to stay for one night at a highly recommended hotel on the outskirts of Baltimore and am shocked to find myself in the equivalent of a glorified retirement community. The modern lobby, with marble, gilding, and plastic plants and flowers, suggests elegance. Elderly tenants, some in wheelchairs, others walking with canes, inch their way in and out of elevators. The hallways are drab. The rooms are cheaply furnished. The Baltimore friends who have advised me on the choice of a hotel—a curator, an editor, a businesswoman, and an art historian who lives in one of the city's most beautiful houses—surprisingly named this one. They described it as "exclusive," "fashionable," "quiet," "lovely." Where, I wonder, are they coming from? Why have they not sent me to the far more interesting, exquisite, and stately neighborhoods of downtown Baltimore?

The next day, walking through downtown Baltimore, I understand the subtle messages my white friends have been trying to send me. I am often the only white person on the street. My white friends, in banishing me to the outskirts of town, were trying to protect me—consciously or unconsciously— from the relentless blackness. Several of them, alluding to Baltimore's high crime rate, warned me not to be fooled by the downtown gentrification. The words "fashionable," "quiet," and "lovely" turn out to be code words, metaphors for the promise of racial exclusivity proffered by the hotel's gated grounds and the two crossed keys of its logo.

W O R D S

Look at the dictionary, a seemingly authoritative source. Under "white" we find "free from spot or blemish," "free from moral impurity," "not intended to cause harm," "innocent," "marked by upright fairness,"; *and then phrases like "white knight," "white horse," and "white hope." "Black" doesn't fare so well: "dirty," "soiled," "thoroughly sinister or evil," "wicked," "sad, gloomy, or calamitous," "grim, distorted, or grotesque." Associated terms include black art (sorcery), black and blue (discolored from bruising), blackball (to exclude from membership), blackmail (to extort by threats), black market (illicit trade), black out (to envelop in darkness), black heat (evil), black day (characterized by disaster), and on and on.**

---

*   William C. Ayers, "Racing in America," in *Off White* (1997).

Code words are all around us these days. When a politician declares that we have to stop catering to special interests and pay attention to the middle class, you know who the special interests are and you know that the color of the middle class—symbolically, if not empirically—is white.*

■

I have heard an educated white woman refer to her husband's black physical education student as a "big, black buck"; I have heard university professors refer to black working-class music as "jungle music"; and I have heard a respected museum director refer to an actress as a "big, black momma." These remarks are different in kind from those uttered in expressions of black racism towards whites. When we are among ourselves we may vent our frustration by castigating whites as ignorant, stupid, dishonest, or vicious . . . We do not, as these remarks do, dehumanize and animalize whites themselves.†

■

It's amazing, [I] sit there, and they think I'm Hispanic . . . You'd be amazed what people are saying when they don't think there are black people in the room. They're like, "Oh I can't stand that black guy." And they'll be saying, "Nigger this, Nigger that." But when the black people are around it's like, "Hey Bob, What's up, bro?" And they play like this nice little role.‡

---

* Stanley Fish, *There's No Such Thing as Free Speech, and It's a Good Thing, Too* (1994).
† Adrian Piper, "Passing for White, Passing for Black," in *Transition* 4 (1992).
‡ An unnamed light-skinned black student at a predominantly white Eastern university, as quoted by Joe R. Feagin and Melvin P. Sikes in *Living with Racism* (1994).

P O L I T E S S E

When white people are disappointed, angry, or confused about the black people around them, they often communicate their feelings and thoughts to other white people through a kind of secret language. I have spoken and have been spoken to in this discreet lexicon of gestures, comments, and facial expressions. Several years ago, at a party in my apartment, for example, I played a few minutes of an extraordinary album of political songs and Negro spirituals recorded by a close friend of mine in the early 1960s. The singer, who was black, sat quietly in the corner of the room listening with the rest of my guests. As most people fixed intently on the music, two of my white guests exchanged glances. One, a blond woman in her early thirties, began to snicker quietly to herself. Her boyfriend, no longer able to control himself, began to laugh.

I wasn't surprised: both people had always seemed uncomfortable with blackness. Both had grown up in white, middle-class, suburban neighborhoods. And at one point or another, both had questioned my interest or tried to dissuade me from my work in race studies. On some level, I understood that their discomfort with the Negro spiritual was not incommensurate with their discomfort with blackness in general. Although their behavior embarrassed me, I said nothing to them, either during or after the incident. I looked over at my singer friend, whose eyes remained fixed on the couple, and could only imagine what she was thinking. Later we discussed the incident. She told me that while the couple's behavior infuriated her she chose not to respond to them rather than cause a scene that might make me uncomfortable.

Lately, I have become less polite about such incidents. While white people expect (and fear) that black people will talk back when insulted in this way, they expect each other to keep silent. We rarely, if ever, call each other on our racist comments or behavior. Why should we, when we have been raised to be indirect about matters of race? We look the other way, laugh nervously, tack on a comment of our own.

White racism is not only protected by this conspiracy of silence and acquiescence, it is perpetuated by this inability, unwillingness, or fear of speaking up. I have heard white people use such expressions as "nigger," "black bastards," "*schwartzes,*" "monkeys," "welfare cheats" to describe certain black people; I have heard them ascribe all kinds of negative attributes to African Americans. In the past few years, I have actively called most of my friends, acquaintances, and associates on these comments. I told them that their racist remarks upset or embarrassed me and that I did not want to hear these words again from them. I asked them how they would feel if they knew one of their

friends or acquaintances had used bigoted language when talking about them. To my surprise, many of these people, while
shocked that I talked back, heard me.

F I R E

My great discovery was that poor people, no matter what color they are, have a hard time. They should stop fighting among themselves and get together. We were having a meeting one night . . . It did deteriorate into Nigger this and Nigger that. I finally said, "I heard all I want to hear. You don't want to talk about welfare rights and decent housing. All you want to do is to sit around and talk about niggers. I'm going home."*

■

You know how we come together in times of crisis. Earthquakes. You see blacks and whites together. Look at the little girl when she fell in the well. I was just as upset about the baby as if it was a black baby. The Lord is saying something to us. We're just not listening.†

* Peggy Terry, a white housewife in Chicago, as quoted by Studs Terkel in *Race: How Blacks and Whites Think and Feel About the American Obsession* (1992).
† Leola Spann, a housing counselor in Chicago, as quoted by Terkel in *Race*.

*And here we are, at the center of the arc, trapped in the gaudiest, most valuable, and most improbable water wheel the world has ever seen. Everything now, we must assume, is in our hands; we have no right to assume otherwise. If we—and now I mean the relatively conscious whites and the relatively conscious blacks, who must, like lovers, insist on, or create, the consciousness of the others—do not falter in our duty now, we may be able, handful that we are, to end the racial nightmare, and achieve our country, and change the history of the world. If we do not dare everything, the fulfillment of that prophecy, re-created from the Bible in song by a slave, is upon us: GOD GAVE NOAH THE RAINBOW SIGN, NO MORE WATER, THE FIRE NEXT TIME!** *

* James Baldwin, *The Fire Next Time* (1963).

W H I T E N E S S

In the late 1980s, bell hooks wrote brilliantly about the concept of whiteness, imploring writers, intellectuals, and academics interested in the issue of race to stop asking so many questions about black people. African Americans, long the victims of discrimination, have always examined the idea, the state, and the status of blackness; they have long written about their vulnerabilities, suffering, and triumphs in the face of oppression and prejudice. Students of race in America, hooks concluded, needed to start asking another question, one directed at the source of power instead of at its victim: "What's going on with whiteness?"

A handful of scholars, many of them African American, began to use "whiteness" to mean the opposite of "blackness," to signify something that was as much cultural as racial. Whiteness implied not a color of skin, per se, but a usually unexamined state of mind and body. Whiteness was a powerful norm that had been so constant and persistent in society that white people never needed to name it.

I used the word "whiteness" myself in the title of a panel discussion—"Dealing with Our Racism: What's Going On with Whiteness?"—which I organized for the School of Visual Arts in New York in 1990.

Ten years later, hooks's question resounds in academia. Though only a few years old, the field of whiteness studies has claimed a great deal of attention as an emerging discipline. Conferences on whiteness abound. There is a Center for the Study of White American Culture, Inc., in Roselle, New Jersey, and a good number of anthologies, scholarly studies, and textbooks on whiteness. Some of these books—David R. Roediger's *The Wages of Whiteness: Race and the Making of the American Working Class* (1991), Toni Morrison's *Playing in the Dark: Whiteness and the Literary Imagination* (1992), Ruth Frankenberg's *White Women, Race Matters: The Social Construction of Whiteness* (1993), Noel Ignatiev's *How the Irish Became White* (1995), Richard Dyer's *White* (1997), and Richard Delgado and Jean Stefancic's *Critical White Studies: Looking Behind the Mirror* (1997)—are groundbreaking, rigorous examinations of white power and privilege that contribute much to the understanding of the origins and perpetuation of white racism.

Others are more troubling. Take, for example, the recent academic examinations of white trash, America's poorest and most disparaged and despised category of whiteness. Many of these studies overestimate what most other white people can learn about their own racism from the white-trash experience.

"Because white trash is, for whites, the most visible and clearly marked form of whiteness," Matt Wray and Annalee Newitz contend in the introduction to their anthology *White Trash: Race and Class in America* (1997), "it can perhaps help to make all whites self-conscious of themselves as a racial and classed group, to bring . . . us one step closer to a world without racial division, or, at the very least, a world where racial difference does not mean racial, symbolic, and economic domination." In other words, because white trash is the whiteness that is consciously identified in racial terms, the people this term describes exist as a kind of racial minority in the white world. The authors see a certain commonality between oppressed whites and oppressed racial groups, one they believe helps to isolate white trash as the only "white identity which does not view itself as the norm from which all other races and ethnicities deviate."

Rather than heightening white people's awareness of their own racism and its motivations, this argument elevates white trash to a racial minority group in need of protection and analysis. Most discussions of white trash subtly exoticize, and, by extension, fetishize, the social issues around white poverty ("trash-o-nomics") and its icons (Elvis, Wonder bread, and trailer parks). White people who are trash are no less racist than white people who are middle-class. Yet the legacy of shared antipathy toward black people, a legacy that underscores the power of racism to cut across class, is far less important to many students of white trash than the need to examine the needs and struggles of another disfranchised group.

The challenge for whiteness studies is how to advocate the idea of whiteness as a useful classification for examining white power and prestige without ignoring its limitations in defining and describing its subjects. The idea of whiteness, like that of blackness, delimits the complexity of our racial identities. The next frontier of whiteness studies is the racial terrain *between* black and white—the blurred racial boundaries, both biological and cultural, that are as much responsible for making us alike as for tearing us apart. "It is what we share racially," the writer Kobena Mercer recently told me, "and not what makes us different, that frightens us the most." Mercer is right. It is the awareness of the blackness in our whiteness, and the whiteness in our blackness, that most confuses us, disrupting our complacent fantasy that our racial and ethnic identities will always be manifest, simple, pure. Whiteness, like blackness, is not an immaculate, concrete truth but a social construction designed to mark the boundaries of race. Rather than attempting to identify what whiteness is, to make it visible so that we can better understand its potency, scholars might well contemplate the value of admitting what it is not.

K I D S

So we learned the dance that cripples the human spirit, step by step, we who were white and we who were colored, day by day, hour by hour, year by year until the movements were reflexes and made for the rest of our life without thinking. Alas, for many white children, they were movements made for the rest of their lives without feeling.

—Lillian Smith, *Killers of the Dream*

In 1994 the photographer and educator Wendy Ewald, working with the Durham, North Carolina, school system, embarked on an experiment designed to encourage classroom discussion of the issue of race. During the preceding two decades, much of Durham's white population had moved to the suburbs, effectively segregating the school system along city and county lines. With the merging of Durham's urban and suburban school systems in 1992, issues of race and racism—issues that were almost never discussed by students and teachers—continued to trouble the city's classrooms. "When the schools merged and class make-ups were going to change," says Ewald, "I started thinking . . . that in order to empathize with people who are different from yourself, you really have to imagine what [their] life would be like."

In collaboration with Cathy Fine, a white fifth-grade teacher, and Robert Hunter, an African American middle-school art teacher, Ewald devised a project to help young people to think empathetically in order better to understand racial attitudes. Students wrote detailed self-portraits; then they wrote self-portraits imagining themselves as members of the opposite race. Ewald photographed the students posing both as their white and black selves, images replete with the clothes and props they brought from home to create their look. Finally, students were given large-format versions of these photographs to draw on and to incorporate some of the ideas from their written portraits. "At first we met with silence," observed Ewald, "then laughter, and finally an enthusiastic barrage of questions: Could they change their names, their families? How could they know what it was like to be of a different race?"

The teachers discovered a fundamental difference between the responses of black students and those of white students. Whereas black children generally had a clear sense of how they were seen by white people and how white people saw themselves, white children often could not see themselves as racially defined beings. "Since white children rarely dealt with the black world's perception of them," says Ewald, "they had almost no idea of how to pose . . . The African American children never needed such coaching." In the end, the project reflected greater social and cultural realities. The black self was all too often articulated as negative, victimized, suffering, or struggling, the white self as simultaneously unremarkable and powerful—a bland and generalized existence that nevertheless afforded students greater health, intelligence, or wealth.

The following are excerpts from the written self-portraits:

Sheldon, Eighth Grade

African American writing as himself and as white self

Me: [1] Funny, [2] Nice, [3] Smart, [4] Playful, [5] Happy, [6] Mad, [7] Angry, [8] Helpful, [9] Sleepful, [10] Handsome, [11] Strong, [12] Tall (as in confidence), [13] Creative, [14] Good Listener, [15] Dependable

White Me: [1] Corny, [2] Smart, [3] Nice, [4] Playful, [5] Weak, [6] Country, [7] Too confident, [8] Too tense, [9] My name "Billy Bob," [10] Get better jobs, [11] Be a vegetarian, [12] Listen to Garth Brooks

Leah, Fifth Grade

White writing as black self

My name is Natasha. I listen to rap. My favorite rap group is Queen Laeta [sic]. My favorite music group is Boyz II Men and 69 Boyz. My hair is wavy and black. My favorite month is December. My best friend has the smallest nose in the world. My favorite state is New Jersey. My favorite color is blue. My favorite movie is *Boyz N the Hood*. I wear Filas . . . I have brown eyes and am very tall. I'm wearing a Walkman, Vans, coat, jeans, and a Woodstock shirt.

Bryan, Eighth Grade

African American writing as white self

If I were white I would be happy all the time. I would like soc-
cer, hockey, and horse racing. My name would be Billy Jay, and
I would wear tight clothing and every time someone walked
past I would say, "Hi, buddy!" I would feel different and I would
be normal. I would have lots of money and a big house. I would
listen to rock and roll. I would have blond hair.

Chris, Fifth Grade

White writing as black self

My name is Jonathan Tarp. I live in Washington, D.C. I want to
be the first black President. I think I can because I'm nice, fair,
and have good judgment, and if I can't be President, I'll be a
cartoonist. My favorite food is pizza. My favorite color is blue.
I'm a nice person. I love pets. I have two albino mice, Pinky and
Brain, a calico kitten, Coco, and two dogs. Their names are
Sparky and Shadow. I can draw good. I have blue-green eyes,
brown hair. I'm about five foot . . . I want to go to Harvard.

Rachael, Fifth Grade

African American writing as white self

My name is Nicole Kimberly Walters. I am sixteen. My hobbies
are listening to rock music and roller-skating. I have long nails. I

like Michael Jackson. I don't like rap. I like reading Nancy Drew. When I grow up, I'll work at an Italian Pizza Ria. People call me names like Snow White. I have rich parents named Michael and Debbie Walters. My sister is Amy, and my brothers are Matthew and Adam. Black people are nice. I have many black friends too. I like going to the mall with my friends . . . I am spoiled. I have long hair.

Zavier, Fifth Grade

African American writing as white self

If I was white, [1] I will change my name to Jonathan on *Family Matters*. [2] People will call me a saltine. [3] I will be a rock star on stage. [4] I will stay in school. [5] Going to funerals will be different. [6] I will like to go to Greek restaurants.

Danielle, Fifth Grade

White writing as black self

My name is Denise Freeman. I'm eleven years old and have seven family members. I'm five feet and weigh seventy-seven pounds. I have two sisters and two brothers. My family is nice. I'm a Baptist. I have green eyes and short black hair. I live in Brent Creek. I like loud music and wear baggy clothes. I like to dance and sing songs on the radio. I hate when people talk behind my back. I also hate when people talk back.

Kenneth, Eighth Grade

African American writing as white self

If I was white, I would look like that man on *White Men Can't Jump*. I would play basketball a lot. I would go to ballroom dances. I would be normal in my personal activities. And always I would jump. I would be normal as a different race. If I were white, I would be rich so no one would know about it. If I was white, I would buy anything I wanted.

WALKING

The convalescent, like the child, is possessed in the highest degree of the faculty of keenly interesting himself in things, be they apparently of the most trivial.

—Charles Baudelaire, *The Painter of Modern Life*

When I was a boy, my father taught me how to walk—not in the developmental sense but in the sense of turning the rather mundane act of putting one foot in front of the other into a conscious act, dense with intention and implication. On the Sabbath and religious holidays, Jewish law forbade us from taking public transportation; so almost every Saturday, after lunch, we would put on our best clothes and walk briskly all over downtown Manhattan. My father would act as tour guide, filling us in on the history of a building or neighborhood or who owned a particular store. Often without stopping, he would single out things for explanation: statues, building ornamentation, commemorative plaques, urban fauna and flora, and even such benign, but no less meaningful, things as garbage cans, phone booths, newsstands, and public restrooms. From my father, I learned how to walk, observe, and analyze the urban landscape.

These Sabbath walks were especially exciting in the summer. We would leave the house early Saturday evening, after a light supper, and walk uptown. One hour after sundown, when the Sabbath was over, my father would take out the dollar bills he hid in his left shoe and treat us to watermelon at the Forty-second Street Automat. Cooled off by our snack and the cafeteria's frigid air-conditioning, we would continue walking, through Times Square and often up to Central Park and even Lincoln Center.

I was always dazzled but also a little intimidated by the lurid nightlife of Times Square—the strip joints, the porno shops, the aggressive prostitutes who came on to my father ("Need some loving, honey?") even as he walked past with his wife and children. We walked briskly, but my eyes caught all the details of the street, from the mechanical fortune-teller—replete with turban and tarot cards—in one store window to the terse news reports making their way across the electronic Zipper that wrapped around the Allied Chemical Tower. Late, sometimes as late as midnight, we would take the dingy, cherry-candy-scented IND subway back to the Lower East Side.

Walking was a way for us to escape from the sadness of our lives—from our claustrophobic, run-down apartment, from the stench of urine that permeated the hallways and elevators of our building, from the screams of our next-door neighbor fighting with her husband, from the sight of the black boy who fell from a roof and died on the pavement outside my bedroom window. We usually headed for bright, upbeat, elegant, or glamorous places: the tree-lined parks near the East River on the Lower East Side; the shady benches and immaculate lawns of Stuyvesant Town, the middle-class, subsidized housing development to which many of our Jewish neighbors had fled during the 1960s; the museums along Fifth Avenue; the fancy shops of Madison Avenue; Central Park; Rockefeller Center; Macy's; Battery Park and the Staten Island Ferry; and Chinatown. Because we could not afford the luxury of eating in a restaurant, we rarely spent time indoors. Walking, we worked up an appetite, so we prepared salami, tuna, or tinned-salmon sandwiches, wrapped in waxed paper, and carried them along with us.

The will to walk is one of the greatest legacies left to me by my father. As an adult, I am unhappy when I am not walking. I feel intellectually bereft, lethargic, dull. Sometimes I walk to escape; mostly I walk to observe and to think. More often than not, I am attracted to places that are far less flashy, or elegant, or touristic than the destinations of my childhood: I am fascinated by apartment buildings, office towers, theaters, storefronts, even slums. I do not look at the things that most people look at when they walk. I am not much of a window-shopper. I am not much of a flirt. I am not much interested in trouble—the sight of an accident, police activity, or bizarre behavior will quickly send me the other way.

The thing that usually catches my eye, that compels me to look, is race. For as long as I can remember, I have been fascinated by the interaction between people of the same and different races: black people, Asian people, Hispanic people, white people—all colliding in the seemingly unbounded world of the city street. It's not that I'm reducing the world in front of me to race but rather that my eyes tell me that race matters, whether I'm walking on the streets of New York, or Newark, or New

Haven, or Houston, or Baltimore, or Chicago, or Scranton, or Washington. The avoidances, fears, the need to evade or approach, the envy, the guilt, the distrust, the discomfort, the fascination and curiosity, and so many of the other emotional and physical symptoms of racial interaction make themselves clear to me each time I walk.

In a sense, I have become a kind of Baudelairean *flâneur*—the anonymous stroller, the passionate spectator who walks through the city observing, looking for the sake of looking, and, in doing so, sees what makes the city modern, radical, new, complex. Unlike Baudelaire's discreet observer, however, I am not looking for the excitement of modern life. Rather, I am searching for the subtle and not-so-subtle manifestations of racial meaning in everyday life. And in the black, white, Hispanic, Asian, and Native American faces—and in the many more faces that remain racially unnamable, testifying as they do to the historical mutability of race—I am confronted by the limitless and complex interrelationships of race. I suspect that I will be looking for these painful, frustrating, confusing, and occasionally heartening confrontations for the rest of my life.

E P I L O G U E
(April 4, 1998)

It is thirty years, practically to the hour, and I do not have a clue. I have totally missed the significance of this day. I check my E-mail and find a message from my friend Ulrick, an artist and architect. He writes that he is off to the airport to catch a plane to Memphis. He plans to go to the Lorraine Motel today, the site where, exactly thirty years earlier, Martin Luther King was killed.

Ulrick's words arouse odd and conflicting emotions: I am excited for him, and am impressed that he thought of going far enough in advance to do something about it. I am also envious of him. I don't know why he is going, but I'm envious. (He made the trip, he later told me, for two reasons: to do background research for the exhibition and memorial to King that he and a partner are designing for the motel, now a national civil rights museum; and to connect with the history of the African American community into which he, a black man born in Haiti, was adopted.) I am frantic. For a few moments, I fantasize that I will call the airport, book a flight (I *hate* to travel by air), and arrive in Memphis in time for the candlelight vigil I imagine will take place later.

That night, unable to sleep, the evening's news reports from Memphis echoing in my head, I get out of bed and go to the living room. I sit in a chair next to a window, and through the silvery, brushed-steel venetian blinds I see two black men standing on the corner, in the glare of a street lamp. They are shouting at each other. "Fuck you," one of them screams. I stop listening, or, more accurately, I allow their voices to become a background for the voice resounding in my head. It is the voice of my mother, thirty years earlier, shouting why Dr. King deserved to be assassinated. I begin to shake, then cry.

I sit in the dark. The voices outside stop. The voice inside my head stops. I start to retrace my steps over the past two years of writing this book. My thinking is ordered and methodical. First things first: Why, from the outset, did I choose to begin this book with my mother's tirade about Dr. King? The answer comes rather easily: her outburst was the primal scene of my awareness of the seriousness of racism. Until that night in 1968, racism had seemed abstract, benign, distant. My mother's harangue made racism real for me in a way it had never been before. Her flaring nostrils, her flushed face, her scowl, her high-pitched screed coalesced into what became my own, private textbook example of the racist. The worst kind of racism was no longer just in Memphis, no longer just in the segregated schools of Little Rock: it was in our living room and there was no way I could ignore it.

EPILOGUE

I walk into my office and turn on the light. I search through my files for the original proposal for the book. I find it and pull it out of its manila folder. As I read—there are five pages—I am surprised at its almost adolescent assuredness, its steadfast belief that white racism can be conquered. The proposal calls for a rather substantial book, linear in its argument and organized into five neatly defined chapters. Instead, I see now, I have written the book in fragments.

I put the proposal back into its folder. I turn off the light. In the writing, I can see the important things my childhood taught me about race. I can forgive my mother for her prejudices. I can forgive my whiteness, too. I suppose that my fantasy about rushing off to Memphis has something to do with this forgiveness, with the need to atone for my mother's sins, and for my own. As I sit alone in my office, in the dark, in the middle of the night, the idea of atonement seems hollow and fruitless. Only the personal, everyday choices I make in the world of racial interactions, and not some abstract or ritualistic gesture of apologizing or of being forgiven, will really make a difference. In the process, I realize, I will always be watching myself.

ACKNOWLEDGMENTS

I would like to thank Jonathan Galassi, my editor at Farrar, Straus & Giroux: his confidence in me and his extraordinary ideas, wisdom, and editorial guidance went far in making this book possible. Paul Elie, who brilliantly guided me through the final editing stages, made many valuable and creative suggestions. Jeff Seroy, both as friend and as director of FSG's publicity office, offered crucial advice and support throughout all stages of researching and writing this book.

I would like to express my deepest gratitude to the following friends and colleagues for their advice, ideas, and support: Donna DeSalvo, Katherine Dieckmann, Patricia Falk, Dennis Kardon, Shelley Lewis, Therese Lichtenstein, Louis LoManaco, Adrian Piper, Elizabeth Sacre, Amy Schewel, Shirley Verrett, Michele Wallace, Simon Watson, Al Weisel, and Patricia Williams. Mason Klein, both as family and colleague, has been there for me in every way imaginable. Finally, I would like to thank my partner, Marvin Heiferman, who not only astutely read and edited the various drafts of this book but remained patient, loving, and understanding throughout the entire process.